BUSINESS BLINDSPOTS

Eliminate Hidden Challenges for Exponential Growth

Doug Winnie

Business Blindspots
Eliminate Hidden Challenges for Exponential Growth

N3 Coaching LLC
6300 West Loop South,
Suite 502
Bellaire, Texas 77401
BusinessBlindspotsBook.com

In Association With:
Elite Online Publishing
63 East 11400 South
Suite #230
Sandy, UT 84070
EliteOnlinePublishing.com

ISBN - 979-8677666896 (Amazon Paperback)
ISBN - 978-1513660479 (Paperback)
ISBN - 978-1513660462 (Hardback)
ISBN: 978-1393774525 (eBook)

Recession/Pandemic BONUS

Implementing the systems in this book
will put you ahead of the competition even during
challenging times.

FREE BONUS

Download the Recession/Pandemic Business Checklist:
BusinessBlindspotsBook.com

Praise for Doug Winnie & *Business Blindspots*

"Doug's writing leverages 10 years of business coaching at ActionCOACH™ and the additional 20 years of owning businesses. It helps everyone easily understand critical business concepts and how to implement these strategies in a way that allows every business owner and every team member to really get it. This is a must read for any business owner who wants to become more successful."

— Bradley J. Sugars, International Best-Selling Author, Speaker, and the World's #1 Business Coach

"There isn't just one area of the business that Doug has helped us in. He's helped us in almost every area and has made a huge difference in the success of the shop. I know that by following the systems and methodologies he's given us, we are way ahead of the competition and worthy of being the prototype store for the entire franchise."

— Mike Simon, Owner, MyShipley Donuts

"This book outlines all that he teaches me and my family about growing a business from a simple start-up to become a very successful and ultimately happy business owner."

— Dr. Marshall Goldsmith, International Best-Selling Author, Speaker, and the World's #1 Executive Coach.

"Having been out of the corporate world for the last 6 years, this has made me realize all the things that I've forgotten. I need to apply myself in many, many different ways."

— Moose Rosenfeld, Owner, Network in Action

"Without the help of Doug and his whole ActionCOACH™ team, there is little chance I would be in business today. He not only showed us how to get our company out of chaos, but to learn how to turn it into a true business. He truly is a passionate and an amazing coach. He really cares deep down about our success and every time we leave his office, we feel like we are helped a little better down the right path to success. Anyone that has the slightest desire to be successful in their business would be crazy not to have Doug and ActionCOACH™ on their team."

— Steve Rozenberg, co-Owner, Empire Property Management

TABLE OF CONTENTS

FOREWORD

Business Blindspots is like being told you're fat when you already know it, and still if no one tells you, denial might be the single biggest reason you don't work hard to lose weight. From a business perspective most businesses know they need more sales yet might not realize the blindspot that prevents sales. Realizing the real blindspot will cause solutions to appear and then action taken causing more sales — all because of awareness of the blindspot.

As a mentor and client of Doug Winnie, I've taught and learned from Doug for many years. His knowledge and experience on the small-to-medium-sized business is amazing and instrumental in the "Mom and Pop" businesses growing to be more than they ever imagined.

Once in coaching my son, Bryan, Doug went through a series of questions and suggestions (this is called coaching by the way), helped Bryan to have an amazing revelation on what turned into a million-dollar win relating to his businesses. Without coaching I am certain that million-dollar reality would not have occurred.

Doug is in my 100 Coaches group, which has more than 16,000 applications. The 100 Coaches Group is my legacy

1

to those who want to help others. I'm teaching everyone in the 100 Coaches Group all I've learned over many decades, and it is all free. The only thing I ask in return is that they provide the same education and mentorship to others when they reach their desired retirement.

All Doug has done to help others continues with this book, *Business Blindspots*. He has built his own multi-million dollar businesses, aided many to do the same for themselves, and now is sharing all the wisdom in his book. Congratulations to Doug for investing the time and energy to create this critical element to aid the business owners and their teams to achieve better results faster.

I look forward to more learnings from Doug and appreciate all he has done for me and my family.

Read this book with intention and you'll generate more profits for any size organization, start-up to multi-national, as every business has blindspots — it is awareness that moves you from denial to action-oriented solutions.

Again, congratulations!

— Dr. Marshall Goldsmith

INTRODUCTION

Having known and witnessed Doug's own personal growth and how he has helped so many business owners achieve their goals I'm excited to share with you the introduction to *Business Blindspots*.

As a serial entrepreneur since a teenager, I've built & sold; bought, fixed & sold; and coached many thousands of businesses. The one I'm most proud of is ActionCOACH™. At the time of this writing, we operate in 82 countries, with nearly 1,000 coaches, and work with tens of thousands of business owners every week, to teach, guide, and hold them accountable, so they can reach their personal success. ActionCOACH™ is where I met Doug when he became one of our franchise partners.

As Doug shared his experiences and challenges, also building & selling businesses, we realized we both started as teenagers. We share several parallels of business, one being we both like to learn and quickly apply what we've learned. It is exciting to see Doug sharing his knowledge and wisdom in this book, *Business Blindspots*, so others can do as he and I've done — learn and apply.

As he describes the Five Pillars of every business, combine it with more than 10,000 coaching hours experience gained as an ActionCOACH™, sprinkle in concepts from our coaching business, and then add what he has learned from Dr. Marshall

Goldsmith, Jeffrey Gitomer, Richard Branson, Les Brown, Jim Rohn, myself, and so many others, you'll have decades of knowledge at your fingertips with *Business Blindspots*. Doug mentions his journey with the ActionCOACH™ community going from the 1,181st coach, to become the number one in only four years, being inducted to the ActionCOACH™ Hall of Fame, and other great awards and in doing so answers the question, "how did you do all that?" Just this one answer (I'll leave you to read it yourself), will give you a huge return on investment (ROI) and return on time (ROT)!

Here is a book that says there are five major components of every business, get good at these five, repeat improving each of the five, and your level of success will only depend on your willingness to keep improving each. There are books on management & leadership, on marketing & sales, and on operations & teams; *Business Blindspots* pulls them all together so every business owner and team member learns enough about each to see their own blindspots, remove them and grow to the level they desire.

One of Doug's quotes: "if the market exists, let's go get it" is why he will be successful with his book. Many business owners don't understand they have blindspots and within a few hours can remove many of them. As Doug says, "knowledge becomes valuable when acted upon." Enjoy the book, and then take massive action. Oh, and after you read this, get an ActionCOACH™ to help guide you and hold you accountable to achieve your dreams!

Bradley J. Sugars
Founder and CEO
ActionCOACH™

HOW TO USE THIS BOOK

This book serves as a checklist, an instruction manual, and a coursebook. Use this book to support all your unique professional situations.

There is something for every business — pre-startup companies to fast-growth companies can benefit. The information here is great for struggling disasters, turnarounds that are overcoming challenges, rebirths reinventing themselves, and consistent, stable growth companies. Whether you are a CEO, a front-line manager, or even a front-line team member, reading and applying the actions in this book can help you and your team drive your company's success.

Many people will find this book useful, so it is most likely not a book to read from cover to cover in one sitting. It may make sense to start at the beginning and read to the end, but determine what works well for you, and feel free to move ahead to chapters that can help you right now.

For example, a discussion on marketing might not have much value if your organization outsources marketing for your firm. So, you might move ahead for now, but return to that discussion when your organization decides to bring marketing tasks in-house or when you create a new company.

Examples of How to Use the Book

Here are some examples of how to use this book in various situations.

Employed and Eager: You want to create a new business and you are nearly ready to do so. You've been an employee all your life, but now you long to pursue your dream of being a business owner.

For you, it is best to read this book from start to finish quickly, yet thoroughly. Do not do any of the tasks at this point. Instead, read the material and develop a clear understanding of what to do in the coming months and years to build a great business.

Start-up: You own or are a member of a start-up business that profits less than $200,000 (USD) per year. Like the Employed and Eager reader, you ought to read this book from front to back to develop a clear understanding of the content.

Afterward, return to the chapter that covers information you believe you already do well. Perhaps, for example, you might return to the operations chapter, because your business, like many start-up businesses, seems to have a good handle on operations.

Complete that chapter's objectives and checklists. Then, once you finish, move to a chapter that discusses an area in which your business could stand to improve. Read that chapter, and then move to the remainder of the chapters and complete them from beginning to end.

Post Start-Up and Not Quite Established: You are out of the gate. You have some momentum. You are working through the technician stage, as referenced in the book *E-Myth* by Michael Gerber. You are aware that you are still the primary technician, meaning you are an expert in the business. Maybe you are the restaurant owner who is still the chef or you are the law firm owner who still does the legal work.

Your business has surpassed $200,000 annual revenues and is likely earning closer to $750,000 or even $1 million per year. You are beyond the eight-person company stage, and you are no longer the do-it-all business owner.

In this case, you might look at the chapter titles and focus on strengthening the weakest areas of your business. Work on each chapter that you believe will create the most significant return on investment (ROI) as fast as possible for your business.

Established: Having established your company, you now have some profits, and you can delegate tasks to the 10 to 100 team members on your staff. You are eager to improve your business, but you aren't desperate, and you don't want to rock the boat too much or too fast.

This book presumably holds the most benefits for people in this category, especially when thinking on a financial basis. Many — if not all — of the sections of this book should help you make a significant impact on the bottom line of your business.

There are benefits from each strategy, whether it is improving the sales process, increasing the raving-fan quotient, adding 10 points to the team engagement score, or opening a new location. Every strategy that your business implements well should translate into dollar signs.

I recommend starting from the chapter on Margins. Next, work on the Marketing chapter to help you communicate with existing customers.

Move to the chapter on Sales to increase your conversion rates and increase your average sales. Then, spend time on the Team chapter to help you with company culture and engagement. Last, but not least, complete the Operations and Finance section.

Employed — A Cog in the Wheel: If you feel like a cog in the wheel of business, you can still have a profound influence at your company. The best place for you to start is with your personal goals.

Do you want to lead your department in the next few months? Do you want to be the CEO of your company? Your goals will help you define your starting point.

If you are not sure what your goal is, read this book from beginning to end and develop a clear understanding of your situation.

Do you already have an objective? Then ask yourself, "In which area of the business do I need to be the expert," and concentrate on obtaining the experience and knowledge to become an authority in that space.

In many large businesses, the sales leaders move up the ranks fast. However, they often are ill-prepared for their new roles, and what they need is a real knowledge of the information in this book. The small business owner has similar challenges in learning what a blindspot is; therefore, this book has great value for small business owners as well.

Book Elements

Objectives: This book includes chapter objectives that reveal what is necessary to be successful in the area of the business you will find in that chapter. This book follows a flexible soup-to-nuts format. It covers the basics and gives you enough details to execute the steps.

There are opportunities to learn additional information about each topic, which may be necessary for you to do to achieve greatness. The need to know the ins and outs of a topic will depend on your company, your role, and your ability to invest more time and more money.

Chapter objectives are simple and straightforward, and even S.M.A.R.T. (i.e., specific, measurable, achievable, and results-oriented with a timeframe).

Checklists: There are checklists to complete to achieve the chapter objectives. A checklist is a "1, 2, 3" or "A, B, C" list of tasks to finish. If the checklist is numerical, you should (and may need to) do the tasks in that order. For example, before you send a direct-mail marketing piece, you must design the advertisement. Thus, the checklist for that task will be in numerical order.

A broader example is preparing for a long road trip. First, you might check the tire pressure and replace the windshield blades. Next, you would probably examine the belts and fill the gas tank or charge the battery. The last steps might be putting luggage into the car, gathering the maps, and driving off.

When tasks have an order of significance, it is best to perform them in a specific order. However, if tasks are of equal importance, a random order can suffice as long as all of the items are complete. So, some checklists are lengthier than others and contain extra detail. Summaries of these checklists are in the margins and referenced both in the Addendum and on the website. Remember that if you see a numerical list, the order is most likely important.

However, if you see an alphabetical list, the order is not important.

Instructions: There are instructions to follow to complete the checklists. There will be no instructions for self-explanatory tasks. If there is room for error or if a lack of instructions could heighten the probability for error, you will find an outline of details and instructions on how to complete the task. In keeping with the road-trip analogy, for example, I would not tell you how to fill your gas tank, but I would give you details on how to select the best vehicle to meet the needs of your specific cross-country journey.

Sources for This Book

The information in this book comes from many sources. It comes from working as an entrepreneur for more than 35 years and spending time learning from business superstars.

These superstars include Brad Sugars, a multimillionaire, entrepreneur, builder of dozens of businesses, and founder and chairman of ActionCOACH™, a global business-coaching franchise of which I am a proud franchisee. Much of this book comes from what I have learned from Brad Sugars and ActionCOACH™.

I built several of my own businesses, and every single one could have benefited from having an ActionCOACH™

Business Coach. When I didn't have a coach, my businesses suffered.

I remember having massive cash flow issues and hiring a consultant to help solve the problem. I paid the consultant more than $30,000 to solve the problem. Hiring the consultant did work out well and save my business. However, the tool that the consultant created over the six weeks of consulting time was a spreadsheet that ActionCOACH™ has in its toolkit and provides to its clients.

When I first saw the ActionCOACH™ spreadsheet, which was nearly the same thing as what the $30,000 consultant gave me after six weeks, I realized I should have had an ActionCOACH™ for a year and received that special spreadsheet in a day. ActionCOACH™ is amazing at helping business owners build a business that will run on a super-profitable level even without the owner present. I'm grateful to Brad and all of ActionCOACH™ for what they teach, what I've learned, and how they guide clients.

Another superstar is Dr. Marshall Goldsmith. Marshall has multiple Ph.Ds. He is a top global coach to many of the Fortune 500 executives, and he has built a coaching program that has certified more than 1,500 coaches. Goldsmith has three New York Times Best Selling books and is ranked by Thinkers50 as the World's Most Influential Leadership Thinker.

I was fortunate and grateful to be selected from 16,000 applicants to be a member of the MG100, a pay-it-forward group of superstars that spent time learning from Dr. Goldsmith before, in turn, paying it forward. Goldsmith's taught the MG100 all that he could, and then, when an MG100 member was ready, he or she would do the same thing pro bono.

Goldsmith's mission was simple: "I want to help successful people achieve positive, lasting change and behavior for themselves, their people, and their teams."

Nearly everything I've learned about leadership and positive role-modeling comes from Marshall, and some of that information is available in this book.

Many other superstars have given me insight and strategies that I use every day. Some of the methods are in this book, and most have become daily activities that I perform. I'll give credit and reference as often as possible.

Others who come to mind immediately include Sir Richard Branson, Les Brown, Jim Rohn, John Maxwell, Alan Mulally, and Dr. Jim Kim. Each of these mentors taught me and led to my success.

My desire to share what I learned from these experts and my experience owning businesses, including my eight years as a Top 10% ActionCOACH™, led me to write this book.

Some things I'll mention have no source, not because I am trying to be the source, but because there are many sources. Also, some of the content is not originally mine.

I'm a believer in learning from others, acting fast on the knowledge, adjusting from failure, and trying again.

I also want to acknowledge many of the MG100 colleagues for helping me to improve The Five Pillars and holding me accountable. I understand more now about my opportunities in life because of ActionCOACH™ and the MG100 coaches program and I sincerely hope every reader of this book takes away new knowledge and uses it to create great opportunities in life.

CHAPTER 1:

HOW I DEFINE SUCCESS

Success, and mastering the art of success, can suggest there is a universal answer; it is either yes or no, on or off, or success or failure. You were successful or you were unsuccessful. This attitude makes it seem as though there is an end to the success trail when you are, as people often state, on the "road to success."

In fact, a recent Google search for "road to success" showed more than 18 million entries. This figure is fascinating, and it indicates that many people believe there is such a road. Furthermore, it implies there are other roads, some of which do not lead to the sought-after end point of success.

It is essential to aim for "success," but perhaps working from an opposite angle would be helpful for some people. Of course, failure is one antonym of success. It indicates the absence of or the inability to attain success. Exploring and learning from failure can help us understand success.

My dad quit school in the 10th grade. He worked at being a business owner his entire life and had a painting company with few employees. He always had cash — not a lot, but some.

Dad worked endlessly, but because of financial hardships with the business, my mom left. Afterward, Dad raised me and my three brothers as best as he could. The oldest child was 13, while the youngest was six.

The business was never successful, and we had to move nearly every year while I was growing up. Dad swallowed his pride, applied for welfare, and worked harder and harder to raise us.

Dad was completely broke when he lost his life due to an accident. He had failed at school, marriage, and business. He just didn't know what he didn't know, and he saw failure more than success.

But failure is not a bad word. Observing my dad's challenges, perseverance, tenacity, and courage, I learned many good things, and now I teach others. For that reason, Dad inspires me every day to keep going, learning, and growing. In this way, Dad succeeded at what was most important, which was raising four boys.

Without being complacent, we can become comfortable with failure and let it guide us to success. Instead of fearing failure, embrace it.

This brief anecdote from my personal life shows how my dad's failures produced success in me and my brothers. Thus, his failures were, from the right perspective, varying levels of success.

The road to success can be winding and elusive. Just as success is not a simple yes or no, failure has layers. One person's failure can lead to another person's success.

First, let go of the notion that success is an on-or-off switch with no flexibility. Instead, recognize that success is, indeed, like a dimmer switch that fluctuates. The journey is not about being on the road to success, but about riding the never-ending roller coaster of ups, downs, curves, and hills. Some days, you're chugging uphill, while other days, you're speeding downhill.

The road to success can be exhilarating, but also debilitating. It can be financially rewarding for the people who pursue it, yet it is available to everyone. Financial success could be the point at which you obtain your personal best in your savings or checking accounts.

When it comes to health, success could be the achievement of running a marathon or completing goals with help from a personal trainer. For professional public speakers like me, success might appear in moments like booking that 100th event and receiving that first (or 100th) standing ovation.

One of my first big successes, from a business perspective, was growing my business from scratch to the point where the company had profits and revenues exceeding $250,000 per month. All the while, I was just employing myself.

It was also the time when I learned to play golf, took more personal vacations, and had an exciting, growing company. I had invested about seven years of hard work and 60-hour work weeks, along with countless hours studying, learning, and practicing how to become a good entrepreneur, a strong leader and, interestingly enough, a savvy finance expert. This story leads my clients to ask about the "secret pill" or the "magic bullet."

How did this success occur? Who was my biggest contributor? Who would I thank most for helping me achieve my goals? What did I learn in the process? What one thing made it all happen? People ask me these questions and many more time and time again. They want to know the art or magic to the successes that I've had. The answer — the single answer in my opinion — is education.

Mr. Brad Sugars, Founder and Chairman of ActionCOACH™, said during a conference one day, "The more you learn, the more you earn." When I first heard that saying, I already had lived it, so it has stuck with me for years. "The more you learn, the more you earn." What a concept! Education is the key to success. It's funny how people use the words "key to success" decade after decade. What many don't realize is once a person is educated, he or she must act. Education becomes valuable when one uses what one learns. In this way, education is the key to success, and then using the key by taking action is when success will occur.

For me, formal education was not as easy to acquire as it is for some people. Having obtained a good high school education about 30 miles west of Detroit in Wayne, Michigan, I earned a scholarship to attend the University of Michigan; however, after only a few weeks in school, tragedy struck during my nighttime job.

I was robbed and shot — yes, with a gun — while delivering pizzas. I was not terribly hurt physically, but mentally, I was shaken. I went from being a good student to a poor student, and in no time, my college education ended before I could take my first exam.

I had failed at college, so I continued working in the pizza business. On-the-job training and learning to be an entrepreneur turned out to be rewarding. In the long run, I learned many things running a small pizzeria business, and I was only 18 years old.

By the time I was 20, I decided to return to college, so I enrolled at the University of Houston. This time, I had no scholarship, and I had no actual way to afford school. Regardless, I forged onward with my "learn-to-earn" experiences.

When some people face an obstacle, they barrel through it once they understand it. For these people, it is as if the hurdle isn't even there. Others, on the other hand, will try to go over it or around it. Some even ignore it. As a business coach, my job is to help people find the obstacle and then work through it.

A typical example is sales. Some people are great at sales, while others are not. You've probably heard the expression "a born salesperson." We all know that isn't possible. No one is born with sales skills.

Undoubtedly, good salespeople acquire sales skills somehow. We could argue that the ability to learn and act on good sales skills is more natural for some people than others, and perhaps it does have something to do with who salespeople are as individuals. At the same time, the environment is a significant factor, and skills often come from mentors and teachers.

The biggest obstacle probably always will be what we don't know. It is never what we already know that stumps us. Instead, it is what we don't know. Therefore, learning what we don't know is the answer to overcoming the biggest obstacle.

But what happens when we need to acknowledge that an obstacle exists? More often than not, one word comes to mind: denial.

Denial is an extraordinarily tricky state. When you are in denial, you don't know how much it is affecting your performance or your success. You don't even know you're in denial, so you don't consider getting out of it.

Overcoming this significant obstacle usually requires the help of another person who can at least tell you that you are in denial. Another way to know you are in denial is if someone asks you a question or you see or hear something that forces you to think in a new way.

Suddenly, a light bulb turns on. Ding!

Your mind says, "A-ha!" You realize that, all along, you had denied the fact that you didn't know what you didn't know. Sometimes, that point is when you seek out a coach or mentor to help break through that denial.

The first step is to figure out what we don't know. For example, many people don't know how to generate leads or how to do marketing.

Facing the Marketing Mystery

Often, people believe marketing is just about creating your brand, making sure people know about you, and getting your name out in the world. I held that belief for a while, and during that time, I applied strategies that sustained those objectives.

At first glance, these strategies appeared to work. Customers knew my name and brand. So did my friends, business partners, and strategic alliances. Still, I could never attribute any sales to my marketing. Consequently, I stopped marketing and stopped branding.

Our sales team continued to do a great job selling, but after a while, I recognized that I needed someone to focus on marketing. I thought, "Why should I do that?" I didn't know what I didn't know, and I now owned a multi-million-dollar business. Marketing to me was something the sales department oversaw. I perceived it as a necessary evil.

I read somewhere that business owners should spend 5 percent of revenue on marketing, so I hired a marketing manager and paid that person a lot of money to do the "marketing." My marketing manager got me on the radio, put up a billboard on a busy freeway, and helped more and more people get to know my name and brand.

Still, I did not see any results from marketing. Eventually, I had to let my marketing manager go, and I again focused on sales. What I didn't know was that marketing is the fuel that grows a business.

Recently, I was listening to a CD of the Month by *Success Magazine*, a great resource for anyone in business. It reminded me that the biggest restaurant in the world, McDonald's, did not become the biggest, because of its product, nor did it become the biggest, because of its management team or its daily operations. McDonald's reached its level of success, because of marketing.

Today, I am a complete believer in marketing, and I understand that marketing for small-to-midsize companies is about getting leads, especially direct leads. Marketing must have a clear and specific offer that is measurable. There should be no guessing or gambling when it comes to marketing.

An example is networking. Some businesses network well, and it pays big dividends. With a specific goal, a detailed plan, and precise actions, networking to generate leads is an excellent strategy.

When there is a goal, such as to obtain 100 leads from networking this year (or month, or day, depending on your networking participation), you will start to count precisely how many leads came to you from networking. Once you know those numbers, you can determine how many leads become sales and calculate the percentage. Within a few clicks of a calculator, you can compute the financial effectiveness of your networking efforts.

The obstacle of knowing what I didn't know about marketing went from complete denial to understanding. I didn't know anything about how marketing worked, but now I know exactly how to leverage marketing to grow a business. Today, I teach more than 50 strategies every week to clients who want to know what they don't know about marketing for small- and medium-sized businesses.

The unknown is the obstacle we can all strive to eliminate by focusing on what is most important today. We must figure out what we do not know today, so that we can learn to continue the journey to reach our potential.

My father often told me, "When you put your mind to it, you can be anything — even the President of the United States." As a result, I always have known that I can be anyone and do anything I want to do. Put your mind to it.

I've gone from pizzeria franchise manager to information technology professional to ActionCOACH™ business coach. Each stage required me to put my mind to it. As I think bigger and bigger, and I learn more about the opportunities that exist today, my mind often runs wild as I try to determine where to focus my attention.

Role models are vital for great success. People learn, grow, and try to make fortunes, yet not enough of those people make use of their access to mentors, who can recount personal experiences and help mentees create positive results faster than ever.

Over the years, I have looked for other mentors in addition to my dad. I realized that opportunities for success are available everywhere and limited only by the way I am willing to focus my attention.

People like Les Brown, Jeffrey Gitomer, and Brad Sugars all have been extraordinary role models for me. Jim Rohn, too, has become one of my favorite role models and teachers. His audiobooks and videos have been great sources of education and motivation in my life. I only wish I had met the man behind the voice.

When I began my business of being a coach and a mentor, I was terrified — scared to death — of public speaking. In my 10-day intensive training to become an ActionCOACH™, we had to present valuable educational material from the stage. I failed miserably at this assignment. I became physically ill and sick to my stomach at the thought of speaking to a group.

During the training, we had a skit to perform as a team. I was nervous about being on stage, so I chose a part that I could play: the family cat. I sat around and occasionally said "meow" while my team members performed broader roles. My minimal contribution to the group was embarrassing to say the least. I have high expectations for myself, but that was the best that I could give in that moment, because I felt such intense fear about public speaking.

After promising myself that I would overcome my public speaking fears, I began studying Jim Rohn's guides. I found his style phenomenal, and I loved his ability to convey a point through anecdotes and humor. Even today, I value Jim Rohn's material, and I wish he could have made even more of it before his passing.

Another great role model whom I respect is Jeffrey Gitomer. This man knows his stuff when it comes to sales, and he teaches it well. Some people take offense to Jeffrey's style, but I'm okay with it. It can be bold, forward, and even harsh. But, the reality is that Gitomer speaks the truth.

Many people don't like the truth. "You can't handle the truth!" That is what Jack Nicholson firmly said in *A Few Good Men*. Does that describe people in general? No, we all can handle the truth, and we all need to know the truth. Not knowing or caring to know the truth is a form of denial.

If we are in denial, we won't know what, how, or why we should improve. Knowing the truth is the first step to improvement. As I've learned from ActionCOACH™, being in denial is a way to be a victim. People don't want to be a victim. Therefore, we have a responsibility not to let others remain in denial, and we must pay attention when others who help us get out of denial.

Once out of denial, people sometimes begin to make excuses or blame other people and difficult situations for the past. These thoughts allow us to continue to be a victim. When we can change our thoughts and habits, we can take ownership of all we do and all that happens to us.

As Jim Rohn says, "In order to attract success, we must be attractive." I believe that means we also must take ownership to become attractive. If we are not attracting what we need or want right now, what can we do to become more attractive in the future?

In my case, I learned that I could become more attractive by becoming a good public speaker. The better I could be at public speaking, the more success I would attract into my life. Facing the fear of being a public speaker was one of the most challenging things I had ever done. It was an intense experience, but I faced that I was in denial about the power of being a great public speaker.

I became a raving fan of Les Brown after I heard his personal story of overcoming difficult circumstances through persistence, determination, and drive to realize the greatness in himself and others. Now, I follow him and take as many classes as I can from him.

I continue to learn from Brad Sugars, the Founder of ActionCOACH™. Every time I talk with him, I find out something new. He is quite phenomenal when it comes to business. He makes things practical and thereby makes ideas easy to implement. Recently, I attended a fantastic workshop where Brad was the public speaker and training coach. He wowed the audience and me with his stories. I often repeat his saying, "The more you learn, the more you'll earn." It is such a true sentiment. When I began learning from Brad and ActionCOACH™, my income increased, and the people I was teaching saw increases in their income as well.

By allowing mentors to guide us, we can access and utilize the knowledge of people who wish us well. Then, we can change our thoughts and habits, and we can take ownership of all that we do and all that happens to us, as well as those around us.

Fear Holds People Back

During my ActionCOACH™ training, I felt terrified of speaking to the audience. But, I realized that the most influential people in the world found success by being sensational public speakers. Most of the best diplomats and leaders in the history books came to prominence, because of their orator skills, which they learned — and so can anyone. This realization jolted me like a train coming to a rough stop at the station. I needed to become a good orator and communicator to increase my success.

That moment was when I knew that I had to face the fear of public speaking that I held. I understood the fear was all about my desire to feel accepted and entertaining, but not to feel judged. The a-ha moment came when I learned from one of my mentors, Traci Duez, that all those fears were about me.

My fear disappeared when Traci asked me, "Is your presentation about you or them, the audience?" As soon as I grasped the thought that it was entirely about them, my fear was gone forever. Now, I'm a good public speaker who is becoming a great public speaker, because when I'm somewhere delivering a speech, I remember that I am there entirely for the audience.

Fearlessness is a concept I can understand now, because I am, indeed, fearless when it comes to public speaking. It isn't about me anymore; it is about my audience. I'm there to teach people how to become more successful, and that's it. Fearlessness is a trait of the successful.

Success Requires Dreams, Goals, Plans (and Action)

Start with dreams. To be successful, we've got to allow ourselves to dream. Think big. Consider what you would be able to do with unlimited resources and what it would be like to do those things.

I went to see Montserrat in Barcelona a while ago. Montserrat is a multi-peaked mountain that is the site of the Benedictine abbey called Santa Maria de Montserrat.

It took about 90 minutes to get to Montserrat from my hotel, and I could only spend a couple of hours exploring before I had to make the 90-minute trek back to my hotel. I thought about how much easier it would have been to rent a helicopter ride to get to and from Montserrat. It would have taken about 30 minutes to get there and back. I would have been able to spend double the amount of time soaking up the beauty of the setting.

Now, one of my dreams is to return to Barcelona one day and take a helicopter ride to Montserrat. I wouldn't worry about the amount of money it would cost. Instead, I would allow myself to experience Montserrat in all its glory.

Dreams lead us to the next step of setting goals. If I use my helicopter idea as a goal, I must come up with the steps necessary to reach that goal. In this case, the steps include gathering the money plus preparing for the time it takes to get to Barcelona and then the monastery. I have specific goals set to reach those targets, so I just come up with milestones to achieve those goals and reach my dream.

The third step is the plan. Prepare for all the steps that you need to take to achieve your particular goals. Write those steps down. The most important part of the plan is thinking it through. Take time to plan, and include details right down to this week's target, which will help you achieve this month's goals that will help you reach next month's objectives and next year's dreams.

A few additional features of my success formula are prudence and focus. Furthermore, I know that successful people are goal-oriented and lead the way that they would like to be led. They are proud of their contribution to the world, because they know it has value. I will cover these characteristics throughout the book, because each one played a significant role in my success.

All my life, I've been "successful" — from preschool to university to jobs. Each step along the way had ups and downs with a varying definition of success. But, I got through every one of them successfully. The meaning of success varies from person to person, and each of us must define it. The bottom line is that we are all innately successful in our ways.

If we want to become more successful, we need to focus on what that increased success looks like for us and then take the actions necessary to obtain our improved level of success. Driving factors for me have included paying my bills, having more fun and traveling the world, owning nice homes and cars, and enjoying a life that is basically budget free.

Lately, as I've helped more and more people to increase their level of success, I've found that changing people's lives for the better has become a high motivator. Listening to people say, "You saved my business," and "You saved my marriage," and "I'm finally making money," is a great reward. Motivating myself by helping others has been massively valuable and an incredible life lesson. A Chinese proverb says, "If you want happiness for a lifetime, serve others."

My parents were entrepreneurs, and like typical business owners, they were busy. A major part of what drives me is my desire to help people not be like my parents. I want to help people go beyond just having a job that they call their business. I want people not to have a business that devours all their time, all their passion, and all their motivation.

Instead, I want people to have a business that they can use as a tool for personal success, wealth, and happiness. It should be a tool that brings them joy, not pain. Their business can become their path to success.

Learn from Me, and Learn from Others

My message is simple. If I can do it, you can, too!

I grew up in a low-income neighborhood just outside of Detroit, Michigan. I went to school in an average public-school system. I experienced various intense ordeals, including the time I got shot. I began working full-time at 17, and I paid my way through university. In college, I even had to file for bankruptcy.

So, I've been both bankrupt and a millionaire. I'm still working, because I love to stretch myself, learn how to do more, and learn how to help others become more successful.

To speak is to lead. I made the conscious decision to become a public speaker when I realized that improving my skills in that area would be life-changing for me. As I mentioned, the most influential people in the world are great at speaking. Great public speakers can become leaders of the world in part, because public speaking, when done correctly, generates trust with the audience. For any sale to occur, the salesperson must establish likeability and trust, and one way to get many people to like and trust you quickly is to speak to groups.

Jeffrey Gitomer once pointed out that if you want to be a great public speaker, you ought to do karaoke. I was skeptical, but he was on to something.

In business, it is critical to build skills, speak to people, help and move others, continue learning, and take action to put your education to use. Above all, becoming a great public speaker is one of the best ways to help others.

Years ago, I took an improv class. I was nervous, but it was an exciting class. The following year, I took acting classes, and I'm sure that one day soon, singing karaoke will be on the list.

Passion drives me, so creating it is a requirement. Creating your passion begins with answering the question, "What is most important to me?" Answer it honestly and thoroughly. The answer must come from deep within you and produce a significant feeling. Define and refine your answer until it is precise in your mind.

For example, if your answer is that family is most important to you, the next question might be, "What about your family is important to you?" You might then say, "I believe that a family that sticks together will always have love." The follow-up question is, "Okay, so you believe that love is the reason family is important to you, so is having love what is most important to you?"

Depending on your thoughts about what is most important to you, there may be a dozen other questions to clarify your true passion. At the end of the thought process, you might be surprised to realize that family, on the surface level, is not your real passion. Instead, connection to people or the ability to help others be more loving and caring might be your real passion.

Of course, your true passion may indeed be family. Perhaps, for example, you see being a great parent as your true passion. Still, you must answer the same questions as everyone else to help you recognize that you feel this way.

The best way to get to the heart of the matter is likely with the help of someone who can ask you questions. With that person's assistance, keep digging and get to the emotion. These are the steps to knowing, believing, and then leveraging your passion.

I discovered my passion by listening to someone else talk about his passion. His specific story was different from mine; however, the way he spoke and the events he shared caused me to think about my true passion and eventually understand it.

I realized that I loved helping people reach their potential by leveraging their business. I enjoyed helping people see that their business could be a tool for more success and happiness. I wanted to help others "be more, do more, and love more" to make the world a better place.

I have faced many of the challenges small- and medium-sized businesses experience or will experience. Something else unique is that I'm now both an executive coach and a master coach, which means I guide executives to improve. Plus, I help coaches learn coaching skills, including accountability, education delivery, and motivation techniques.

When you combine that with my experience, knowledge, and passion, I am genuinely one of the best coaches on the planet to help others master the art of their unique business success. I'm grateful to have had these experiences, and I'm excited to share more of my knowledge, wisdom, experiences, and journey with you.

I hope you find it valuable as you continue your incredible journey. As I learned from Dr. Marshall Goldsmith, one of my mentors, take what you need and leave the rest.

History Does Repeat

Having coached leaders from more than 300 companies and built seven businesses of my own, I have seen certain things happen over and over again. I wish I had understood earlier that history repeats itself. Unfortunately, I did not comprehend it until I began teaching and coaching, which I started doing during my seventh business. Yet, many concepts do not become valuable or even apparent until we start to teach them.

The concept that history repeats is there for us to see when problems arise. However, many people miss or ignore it.

History repeating isn't considered even when we let go of yet another team member who did not meet expectations. History repeating isn't apparent even when we discover yet another employee drinking on the job. We feel déjà vu when we are upset, because the marketing company we paid fails to deliver results and leaves us questioning the role of marketing altogether, but we don't see history repeating.

Whether it's a history of losing clients or market share or company value, businesses need to realize and remember that there are examples of history repeating itself everywhere, but many people do not realize it. What's more, some people realize it yet don't make adjustments.

But sometimes, people create new rules after they feel enough pain.

People usually create rules, because someone did or might do something wrong. Frequently, people make rules, because a wrongful action occurred and was severe enough that a department or business owner decided that a rule would be the only prudent measure to keep history from repeating.

Occasionally, people create rules after performing a thorough root-cause analysis that exposes a deeper issue that justifies the need for a rule. We often see this activity happen in government, where case studies and legal situations lead to the addition of laws. Someone does something wrong, so the government passes a law to protect everyone else from the same problem.

It's the same in business. As one of the leading business coaches in the world, I see dozens of businesses struggle with the same issues every quarter of every year.

When business owners work on the sound fundamentals that are true in every business, their disastrous failure rate will slow down, turn around, and improve. Statistics show that more than 80% of start-up businesses fail within five years. Among the businesses that sustain themselves for five years, half will fail in the subsequent five years. That means nearly 90% of all businesses will call it quits and close their doors within 10 years.

Some of these businesses fail, because there is no market — or not yet a market — for their product or service. You might say these businesses were "before their time." However, those businesses make up a super small percentage of the total number of failed businesses.

So, if history repeats and every business follows the same challenges, why is there such a low chance of success? I believe it is because of a couple of things, which I will describe in this book.

Knowledge is everywhere. There is an unlimited amount of business books for most industries, and these days, the quality of information available is high. What's the issue, then? Why do we have access to this knowledge, but still see low success rates?

What we need to do first is understand that knowledge has value when we act upon it. Reading this book and then doing nothing will be a waste of your time. Take the information available here and put it into an actionable plan.

Before reading even one more paragraph, commit to taking notes. Then, take daily steps closer and closer to financial freedom, which you will find as a result of having a great business.

The late, great Jim Rohn explained it best, saying, "With a job, you can make a living. With a business, you can make a fortune."

I also love the thought. "Why don't you have the $500 pair of jeans? It's not because you don't deserve them. It's because you can't afford them."

Why don't you fly first class everywhere? Because you can't afford it. Why don't you have a $75,000 BMW? It's because you can't afford it.

I hear you when you say, "It's just a car," or "It's just a piece of clothing," or "Those are just material things."

You want to cure a disease, donate to charitable organizations, and save the world. Well, I am here to tell you that you can do all those things and more when you are wealthy. Of course, money doesn't buy happiness, but it does provide you with options and opportunities.

Brad Sugars tells the story of being a teenager and wanting a new pair of trendy jeans. At the time, he was wearing corduroys, a typical style of pants in the 1970s and 80s. They were practical and inexpensive, but not what Brad wanted. His parents said no to the jeans. They told him he would be fine wearing the corduroy pants he already had. From that point on, Brad promised himself not to let anyone ever limit his ability to buy something he wanted.

By Brad's 25th birthday, he was a millionaire. Now, Brad can buy subdivisions with cash, though he would use low-interest loans as smart leverage. He lives in a 33,000-square-foot mansion in the hills of Las Vegas and owns every car he wants, including a gorgeous midnight-blue Rolls Royce convertible. He can travel anywhere anytime, and it is all because he uses his understanding of business and acts on what he learns each day.

One of his famous quotes is, "The more you learn, the more you earn." He is living proof that knowledge has excellent value when you act upon it. The reality is that wealth provides options, and those options can be limitless.

With financial freedom, people suddenly have options like choosing to own a BMW or Mercedes or Jaguar, or buying one house or five houses, or taking a weekend vacation to the nearby beach or a full trip around the world. Wealth also provides for the ability to help others through charities, foundations, churches, and communities.

Rotarians are a great example of a group of people who help many unfortunate poverty-stricken groups around the globe. Rotarians, on average, have limited time and finances, so it can be challenging for them to make donations beyond $100 or so at a time. There are 35,000 Rotary Groups worldwide. At the time of this book's publication, there are 337,842 members in North America and 1,189,466 worldwide. The organization provided $101.5 million in monetary aid in 2015. This number equates to $85.33 per Rotarian.

Why can't this group of dedicated professionals donate lots of money and time? They can't afford it. The same goes for every unsuccessful business owner. Rotary is a great group, and everyone should be a member. It would be much better if the average donation were 10 times the amount today. Again, knowledge becomes valuable when acted upon.

A Client Story

A couple of years ago, one of my best clients told me about an employee who was performing poorly. Inspection of the company vehicle uncovered old, dirty uniforms, and under that pile was a well-hidden fifth of Jack Daniels whiskey.

The employee had been drinking while on the job, possibly while driving, and was unquestionably intoxicated while working at clients' homes. The client terminated the employee and encouraged the person to find a treatment program. During the clean-up of the truck and the client projects, it appeared the employee also was stealing business and doing work for cash on the side.

There always had been a drug-and-alcohol policy forbidding the consumption of alcohol during working hours. However, there had been no enforcement of it nor even a way to check on it. The company updated its policy and insisted upon each truck receiving a deep clean each week by another staff member from the one who used it all week.

Regardless, the same thing happened again with a different employee. Lack of enforcement and accountability caused history to repeat itself. So, the client implemented a one-strike, zero-tolerance drug-and-alcohol policy that included a random testing process.

Because of the repeated occurrences, the client learned a lesson and took action. Now, by applying the rules and following the philosophy of putting education into action, the client has begun to resolve the problem, which should decrease and eventually disappear.

Simple or Complex

Concept: A complex business and a simple business are almost equal except for one difference, which is the number of Pillar sets.

For example:

Let's say we have a pet golden retriever named Max. We got Max as a puppy when he was just eight weeks old. He was the cutest thing on the planet at that age. Max is like a start-up business that is exciting and even fun at the beginning. We train Max to go potty outside, and it eventually works; however, there always seems to be something else to teach him. Just like a start-up business, Max requires ongoing attention, and his learning never seems to end.

The simple company is like having one pet. There is still a lot to do and teach, and there comes the point when owning Max seems pretty straightforward.

Owning a complex business, on the other hand, is like owning a zoo. You have Max, but you also have many animals under your care. Each animal has a special diet, feeding schedule, exercise program, and medical plan. There are too many animals for just one zookeeper to manage, so you must hire a large team.

Having only one pet is simple, while having an entire zoo is complex. To-do lists for the animals are categorically similar, but the content in those categories and on those lists is different.

A complex business is the same. Each area of the business is identical to the others in terms of the to-do list categories. However, the content within those categories and lists is different.

So, can we agree a complex business is equal to a simple business except there is a larger quantity of the same types of lists?

Here is a list of items, which belong in the single business and in each of the divisions or areas of a complex business: a marketing plan, a sales system, a product or service to sell, an operations plan, financials, and job descriptions.

A simple business and a complex business have the same categories, which is why it is an easy concept for businesses to buy other companies and merge them into a new company. Then they can eliminate duplicate functions, which will save the merged company money and, in the end, justify the purchase from a return on investment (ROI) perspective.

Learning from Others

Consider what it would be like to go to school, kindergarten through 12th grade, and spending time in a classroom without ever having a teacher.

In the classroom, you would have access to a chalkboard with chalk and an eraser. There would be other supplies and even books and toys.

Like most people, you would be interested in the items around the classroom, and you would play with them. After some time, you would figure out that you could use the chalk to write on the chalkboard, and that you could use the eraser to remove the chalk. You would be fascinated, and you would make use of what you learned.

Eventually, you would become bored and stop going to the classroom. Years would go by, and you would sometimes think about school and question its purpose. You would wonder if there were any other lessons you could have learned from that room.

This is how things could have gone without a teacher. It would be similar to the methods cavemen used in prehistoric times.

Of course, that is not how we learn today — at least not when it comes to formal education. Each level of education has a specific teacher to help students learn about available tools and how to use them. Each level contains goals and new layers of personal growth.

Initially, the teacher shows students how to communicate. Then, the teacher helps the students improve their communication skills. We learn to use our voices. We learn to read. We learn about non-verbal gestures and spiritual, emotional methods of communication. The use of each tool is essential to our future ability to work with other people.

Many people learn to start a business with little or no mentorship. They go to the classroom. They experiment with the supplies. They know the basics, but they need a teacher to get to the next level.

Business coaching fills that void, and the business coach becomes the mentor for your business classroom. Business coaching provides a clear path and a specific education process that you can use as a business tool.

It takes about seven years to create a fully functioning multi-million-dollar business when you follow the proper evolution of growing a business.

There are thousands of tools a business owner can use. Some have helpful directions, and others do not. A business coach selects the right tools and teaches the business owner to use them to achieve a proper return on time (ROT).

The Five Pillars

Every business follows this same model. Most big companies do it well and still make mistakes that are sometimes fatal. Almost all small companies neglect to pay attention to what a business coach can cover, and they join the 80% of businesses that fail in the first five years.

Marketing, Sales, Operations, Finance, and Team are the Pillars upon which you can build a successful business. When each of these Pillars is equally successful and gets equal attention, a company will grow until failure occurs at a level that prevents growth, or until the market changes and the business misses its chance to pivot.

The Five Pillars, the channels of a business, each require significant attention at varying stages. The Five Pillars are simple in and of themselves, yet it is challenging for business owners and leaders to keep them simple.

When I reflect on how I built a couple of my businesses, I see how I was a business owner facing those challenges, but didn't know it. Now, I can see my mistakes with perfect 20/20 vision, and it is easy to separate the positive from the negative.

I don't think my case is unique either. Back then, I had just as much training on how to grow a business as the next business owner facing challenges.

But now, my past successes and failures are glaring. I needed marketing. I didn't learn fast enough, and I undervalued teamwork. I should have kept a closer eye on my finances, and my sales systems were non-existent.

On the other hand, daily operations were pretty good. In fact, the area that I developed and delivered best was the Operations Pillar. This area tends to be what most start-up businesses do well before anything else.

My last "good" business was a technology firm. We started as a one-person company, meaning it was just me, and we grew to 64 total full-time teammates. We earned as much as $250,000 in profits per month and lost as much as $85,000 in a month.

We opened offices in three cities in the United States and failed to make profits in two of them. We hired and trained great team members and had to lay off 40 people in one week due to poor sales — or no sales — after the technology bust.

Looking back, I realize I acted too slowly to adjust to the market conditions. I failed to watch the losses build, and I didn't consider how marketing would affect sales. Also, I didn't keep our biggest customers happy when I could have, which would have reduced the number of layoffs.

Although I had consultants giving me some assistance, I didn't have a business coach to advise me on the right plays to make, like a sports coach would help an athlete. Now, I am a business coach, and my failures are more important to my clients, as experience and education are invaluable.

Important: Do you have a job, or do you have a business? Of course, if you are the business owner, then you own a business, so the answer must be a simple one. Or is it?

Consider these additional questions: Have you ever had a business valuation performed? Do you plan to sell your business at a certain point? Is it okay if you don't get a paycheck due to cash flow or lack of profit issues? Do you have employees? Do you look at your profit-and-loss (P&L) statements in accrual form?

If you answered yes to all the above questions, then you are a business owner. If you answered no to most of them, you are likely the owner of a job that you created by starting a business. This clarification is critical. You may find this topic sensitive, and you may even disagree with me on it. Still, I encourage you to read on and see if you can understand my point.

Jim Rohn says, "A job will make you a living. A business will make you a fortune." Did you build a business to have a job, or to make a fortune?

Many people started a company to have a job. Maybe their former job laid them off or fired them, or perhaps they quit. Whatever the reason, they needed income and decided to control their destiny. Good for them. I say, "Congratulations and welcome to the world of owning a business."

As you have most likely discovered, there are many challenges to overcome when you begin — or want to begin — a business. Your first challenge is usually to get sales. Some people are fortunate enough to receive sales

CHAPTER 1: HOW I DEFINE SUCCESS

from their former workplaces, and others are just in the right place at the right time.

However, most people are not as fortunate. Besides, a business owner will always focus on getting more business anyway, no matter how lucky he or she was in the initial days of the company.

If you are a business owner, you want to have more income and more teamwork, so that you can make a fortune. If you own a business and are focused on making an income, especially one that just pays the bills, you likely have a J.O.B., which according to my ActionCOACH™ education, stands for "Just Over Broke." Depending on your motivation — to pay the bills or to make a fortune — you understand the importance of learning. You see the need to hire others to do many — or all — of the everyday tasks in the business.

When you first start, you are the Marketing Manager, Director of Sales, Chief Operations Officer, Webmaster, VP of Finance, HR Director, General Manager, CEO, and Controller. You wear all the hats. You take on every role even though you don't have all the necessary skills to do so.

Consider a locksmith named Jack, who works every day to install, repair, and re-key locks. We'll call his company Jack's Locks. Jack has a business, and that business is to be a locksmith.

Jack's Locks doesn't have many employees, and Jack is forever the locksmith. When it is time for Jack to retire, he may give the business to one of his children, or maybe sell it for a minimal amount. Then he will live out the rest of his years in a semi-comfortable state.

However, Jack never will have enough money to travel the world and enjoy a non-budget lifestyle. Instead, he will have a lifestyle that forces him to sit at home and watch the world go by, and he will always have a budgeted lifestyle. These conditions are the result of having a J.O.B., and Jack will be just over broke his entire life.

This same locksmith business with the same business owner can have a different focus and a significantly different outcome. Imagine Jack owning a second version of the locksmith business that has a better focus. We'll call this business Premier Locks.

Jack and his leadership team focus on growing Premier Locks into a great business that can run without their constant supervision and then sell when they reach 55 years old. This business has several locksmiths on staff, and the owner, Jack, is the teacher, motivator, and leader of the organization.

Jack's focus in this business is to grow the business and make profits that he can reinvest in the company. In this way, Jack can build a cash-flow machine and set himself up for a different lifestyle from what we saw in the first example.

CHAPTER 1: HOW I DEFINE SUCCESS

Plus, this business has the goal to sell for $5 million in 10 years, and that allows for this owner to make a fortune. Remembering this goal, Jack always remains keenly aware that his business is, in fact, an investment strategy.

The big difference between the J.O.B.-business owner and the business-business owner is their goal. One person wants to earn a wage, while the other wants to make a fortune. This book is about building a business that has all the Five Pillars, not just one, which would limit people to the goal of having a better job.

The Five-Legged Stool

How many legs are necessary for a five-legged stool to stand? One broken leg would leave four legs, and that might work; it would not work as well as if all five legs were useful, but it would still work.

If the right three legs remained, the stool might be okay most of the time. But if there were only two legs or one, the stool would be unable to stand. Without a minimum of three legs, the five-legged stool would fail. With three, four, or five legs, the stool could do its job.

In the same way, it is only when all Five Pillars of a business work well that the business can grow — and grow to almost any size.

This book will describe each of these Five Pillars, which are marketing, sales, operations, finance, and team. Being an expert on one Pillar and average or mediocre when it comes to other Pillars will stunt the growth of your business.

Think of the length and strength of the stool legs as equal to the quality of the Pillars. A weak leg is an inability to sustain extra weight on the entire stool. A couple of weak legs can mean danger, and three weak legs equal a possible crash when you add pressure to the stool. This same thing happens in business.

Let's do a quick exercise. See the table that includes the chart with the scale from 1 (weak) to 10 (strong). How would you quickly score your business Pillars?

Are your Pillars somewhat equal in strength? Every business I've coached has had at least three Pillars working. On occasion, those three Pillars even work well. Still, those businesses hit a ceiling or a limit on their growth. As we work to focus on the weakest Pillars, they begin to grow again.

Here are a couple of examples. Consider my client, who owns a dental practice. This business has one dentist, the owner. It has a receptionist and a dental assistant on the payroll, and for a long time, the dentist's spouse ran the marketing, sales, and finance Pillars.

Unpaid spouses are a terrible idea, by the way. Would you want your spouse to work without pay for someone else? Yes, I realize it seems like an investment of time for future rewards. However, if you must employ an unpaid spouse, friend, or relative, consider using this model for only a short time of maybe 90 to 120 days, and then pay them something. A business that runs on free labor is a volunteer organization, not a business. Also, the longer the free labor exists, the more the habit becomes ingrained in the business model and keeps the Pillars weak.

At the dentist's practice, my client was a phenomenal dentist (i.e., operations) and did a decent job generating leads (i.e., marketing). The small team did a great job of getting new clients in the door, which was sales, because it turned a lead into a patient.

When I started helping this business, it had two weak Pillars: finance and team. Finance was weak, because the business had minimal cash to keep the business open and running, and it did a poor job of training and empowering its team.

Now, a business can operate with three of the Five Pillars intact. The challenge becomes how well those Pillars can handle the stress of growth.

As the dental practice and I worked together, I realized the business was accidentally exaggerating the strength of its sales. The spouse was making sales after the dentist analyzed what patients needed for the health of their teeth. The expert about the needs was the dentist, while the person selling was the non-expert, unpaid, low-credibility spouse. These circumstances resulted in an ability to get clients, but not revenue.

Eventually, the spouse took a paying job outside the dental practice, because the family needed additional income. The dental assistant became the new salesperson, which meant the salesperson was still less qualified and less credible than the expert.

The business is still open, but barely making ends meet. It is decreasing its marketing budget, because of a lack of funds. The five-legged stool is weak. Three of the Five Pillars of business — sales, finance, and team — are working ineffectively, so ultimately, the business could fail.

The rest of this book will illustrate the Five Pillars in detail. You also will find stories of clients who either "got it" and worked to strengthen the weak Pillars or didn't make a change and experienced negative consequences.

Mindset or Skill Set

Our thoughts are pretty much all we have. Sometimes, we are better at letting others control our thoughts than controlling our thoughts ourselves.

Think about the TV you watch. I was talking with a fellow networking buddy, and he told me about his morning ritual, which included watching at least 30-minutes of Fox News every morning. What do you think? Does watching

Fox News help you create thoughts of your own or give you thoughts based on its news programs?

Imagine you have a big sales presentation coming up in a few hours. Your morning ritual informs you that the economy is bad, the housing market is bad, taxes are going up, and elementary school care is falling behind.

You learn about a car accident on the freeway and an auto-manufacturer recalling 100,000 vehicles, because the engine light flashes at random times in some models.

Maybe you are lucky enough to hear how the weather will be stellar over the next few days. Then the forecaster says something like, "Great weather today. Too bad most of us will be at work and won't get to enjoy it. Have a great day anyway!"

Outside entities have put these negative thoughts into your mind. You might be able to ignore those outside entities. Some people think they ignore them well. However, many other people admit that ignoring negativity is a challenge.

If your attitude is everything, as sports coaches sometimes maintain, and controlling your attitude is key to having a positive outlook, why do we allow negative thoughts into our minds?

We do it, because we are human, and we want to be aware of all the threats around us. Our mind is always looking around for threats so that it can protect us. We look for problems, even seek them out, and then work to combat them or defend ourselves. We still stop and look at the freeway accident, because as humans, we are drawn to negative drama.

So, if you've absorbed negativity first thing in the morning, your mind is working hard to protect you from problems. If you have a presentation to give, are you better or worse off for having looked at this information? It's most likely the latter, of course.

Your tendency to focus attention on negativity could contaminate your attitude during your sales presentation. You may even talk about the negativity in the world with your colleagues before the meeting. Maybe you will even mention it to your clients during the presentation.

Zig Ziglar calls this "stinking thinking." We should avoid it at all cost, and avoid it is exactly what I do. I don't watch the news, I don't read the newspaper, and I don't listen to the "stinking thinking" out there in the world. Instead, I listen to audiobooks on sales and motivational talks by great business leaders like Jim Collins, who can tell me about the journey from "Good to Great."

What has been the result of avoiding all this negative input? In the past decade, I have gone from the bottom of the ActionCOACH™ community rankings to the top. I've gone from having no awards to winning the most prestigious award. I've helped my clients think positively, and they've won awards, too. Plus, they have grown their businesses.

So, how do we keep those negative thoughts off our minds? The first step is to realize that they don't have to stay. You don't have to keep a thought.

It's true. Every thought you have is expendable. This skill is one we can all have. I've been working with my "thought coach" for many years, and it is incredible how quickly I can throw away a negative thought.

You can check out what my thought coach does by visiting her website[1]. I highly recommend taking her online profiling test and learning from her and her team. I found it amazing to see what I didn't know about my thoughts, and those areas could be blindspots for you as well. The more blindspots we remove, the more successful we become.

The bottom line is that you can, indeed, throw away a thought. For example, if someone cuts you off on the freeway while you are driving to work one day, your first thought might come from a space of anger. However, you can say to yourself, "I don't want to keep this thought."

You ask yourself, "What is my next thought?" If this thought also carries anger with it, you can again tell yourself to throw it away and ask, "What is my next

---

[1] BreakFreeConsulting.com

thought?" Follow this conscious thought pattern until you reach a thought you want to keep.

After a while, you might say, "He probably didn't see me. It's a good thing we both kept safe."

You decide to keep that last thought, and your drive continues, unhampered and free of grief or guilt. Over time, you can develop this skill and begin not to notice negative thoughts in the first place. These days, I don't even perceive negative thoughts, because my mind automatically follows the conscious thought pattern of searching for a positive thought to keep.

Thoughts are fascinating. Your job is to pay close attention to the thoughts that you allow to spend time in your mind. Then, decide what to keep. If you do this for 30 days, you'll begin creating great habits to have positive thoughts and a happy, more successful life.

Now, I will discuss my experiences and thoughts on mindsets and skillsets. I will share some of the things I have found to be vital in both life and business. To begin, I would like to pose a couple of questions for you.

Which is more important, mindset or skillset? How do you have the most productive life and lifestyle when working on your mindset or your skillset?

Do you want to achieve more? I'm going to assume you do, because you are reading this book. Let's just start with the concept of achieving more. Do you consider it to be a mindset opportunity or a skillset opportunity? Usually, when I ask clients this question, we agree that it is about mindset.

So, I want to talk a little bit about a concept called neuroplasticity. If it sounds too scientific, don't worry; I have good news. You may not know it, but you are already an expert.

Neuroplasticity describes how experiences reorganize neural pathways in the brain. Long-lasting functional changes occur in the brain when we learn and memorize new information. These changes are what we call neuroplasticity. Part of neuroplasticity is the ability to build and eliminate thoughts. Think back to high school biology classes on how the brain works.

The brain is an electrical instrument, and it is going to follow the path of least resistance. When you think of the brain, think of it as a circuit port. It is going to build and follow a path. Unlike a circuit board that is unable to change, architect the circuit board, and the next thing you know, it will do what you expect it to do over and over again.

Our brain does not necessarily work that way, but we can build neural pathways and prune them. From before birth, we create neural pathways and improve them. Think of the neural network like the roads in your town. Someone designed the roads and decided where they should go, and over time, they built new roads and took down old ones. The brain works similarly, but instead of roads there are neural pathways.

You may have heard the saying that human beings are creatures of habit. While this may be true to a certain extent, the reality is that we are all creatures of imitation, and we create neural pathways through imitation.

No matter where you are from, you likely have some form of accent. If you are from North America, perhaps you have a Canadian accent or an American accent. If you are from Australia, you might have an Australian accent. No matter where we are from, be it Asia, Europe, South America, or anywhere else, we seem to think that we were born with an accent.

In reality, we were not. We created our accent through imitation. We heard the people around us speaking the same way, and by imitating them, we formed a habit of using this particular accent, too.

Also, people can learn a new accent. Many famous actors and actresses learn to do so for roles all the time.

From the time of a person's birth, his or her brain is a manufacturing system that builds neural pathways just like an architect designing roads. It goes through a rapid stage of construction. There must be some architectural system inside the brain as well. This system is that imitation system. It's listening, watching, learning, and paying attention, and it becomes the architect that starts building things. The next thing you know, you end up with these neural pathways, and they become a habit.

We are creatures of habit, but remember, we are creatures of imitation first. So, who are we imitating? Who is the real architect? We imitate everyone around us — parents, teachers, siblings, children, clergy, newspapers, TV shows, politicians, leaders, bosses, coworkers, and even advertisers.

It continues this way throughout your entire life. Sometimes, we even learn fears from our role models. We learn limitations from them, too. Some opportunities come from architects as well.

Speaking of fear as something we acquire from our architects, or role models, the fear of public speaking is something we might learn from other people.

Do you think we were born with this fear? Of course not.

Scientists say we were born with three specific fears. One is the fear of loud noises, such as a loud crack of thunder that startles us and makes us jump. Another innate fear is the fear of abandonment. When we're born, we need other people to care for us. The third fear is the fear of being dropped, which turns into a fear of heights for some people. According to scientists, those fears are the only ones we have at birth. Notice how the fear of public speaking is not among them.

Often, public speakers go on stage and don't appear to fear it. But, as we discussed before, I used to feel terrified by public speaking. Today, I feel more comfortable with public speaking, because I worked hard at conquering that fear. The neural pathway that once existed is now gone, and in its place is excitement about public speaking. It excites me, because I know it is a chance to help as many people as possible.

You have neural pathways that help you, and I guarantee, you also have neural pathways that are holding you back. They exist. During the years that I've been working with ActionCOACH™, I've seen people's limitations every day.

We call it self-limiting beliefs. There are neural pathways in each of our heads, and they prevent us from doing more.

Here are a couple of other neural pathways that you might have as well. Maybe one was you must go to college and get a job. Who helped architect those particular thoughts for me? My parents did. They were not wealthy, and they did not have much success. They never would admit those things, but it was their reality, and I realized it as I grew up. They told me not to be an entrepreneur, so that was a neural pathway that I created in my head.

They even told me not to own a business. Today, I own four businesses, and I've had nine businesses in total. Three of those businesses have become multimillion-dollar companies, and two I have sold. Now, I have a multimillion-dollar action approach toward business in America.

Sometimes, things our parents or guardians tell us not to do are what we decide to do after all. Why? It's because we still build a neural pathway. Even though my role models said not to be an entrepreneur, my brain did not understand my parents' negative statements.

If you were to have the worst nightmare of your entire life, you would hope not to have it again, right? Parents and guardians don't want children to have nightmares, but the reality is that people will experience nightmares no matter what.

They also will have dreams. It's natural. The brain absorbs information, and it replays a tape to sort out the emotions and ideas. So, if a child watches a scary movie, he or she builds neural pathways around the feeling of fear, and the brain uses those neural pathways later during sleep.

The same happens with the desire to start a business. Industrious people build neural pathways on business ownership, and these lead to the desire to become an entrepreneur.

My dad frequently said, "An A- is a bad grade when a person could get an A or even A+." This concept created within me a need to be perfect. Such a notion is detrimental for entrepreneurs. If growing a business required perfection, entrepreneurs would never move beyond the first steps of opening a business. Even today, I have to wonder, "What is the first step?"

Perfectionism haunts me to this day, and it's all because an influential person in my life placed an idea in my head. The idea grew and grew until it created a perfectionism complex that I might battle forever.

The thought that a lot of us has is that entrepreneurship is too expensive. What is it that is too expensive in this world? Maybe you think a $1,000 pair of jeans is too costly. Who told you so? Who has your ear?

Maybe instead of a $1,000 pair of jeans, it's a diamond ring that costs $200,000. Who told you it's too expensive?

According to my mentors nothing is too expensive. Instead, it's that you can't afford certain things right now. But you could work to afford them, so they are not too expensive.

However, we get caught thinking things are too costly, and we don't need anything with a high price tag. It's not that you don't need these things that you desire. It's that your brain is telling you those things are too expensive.

We can create new roads to replace the old ones. All we have to do is start to think about how to build new roads?

Where are we going to find the right architect? The right architect is the one that's going to build the roads you want, not the roads that someone else wants. You are it. You are the architect.

Brad Sugars and the ActionCOACH™ team created something called the formula for success. It looks like this:

Dreams x Goals x Learning x Planning x Acting = Success

We need to learn how to create a strong mindset with beneficial strong neural pathways to see this formula through. Here are a few ways to build such beneficial neural pathways. These are not in any particular order, and it is vital to do all of them.

The first thing to do is to start speaking in what are called "I am" statements. I learned this strategy on my first day of ActionCOACH™ training. It is a simple approach that we can develop over time.

"I am" statements are positive affirmation statements about the things we want to do or are in the process of doing, and we say them first thing in the morning when we wake up. We also repeat them out loud before you go to sleep.

An example might be "I am a great business owner." It could be that simple. It could be a little more sophisticated. It could be "I am a fantastic business owner who employs hundreds and thousands of employees and influences tens of thousands of people in my industry."

It could be more sophisticated than that, or it could be as straightforward as saying, "I am a proud parent," or "I am a valuable member of my community."

When I joined ActionCOACH™, I promised to try "I am" statements even though I had never heard of them. The first night's homework was to create 20 "I am" statements. The instruction was just to say them. So, I did. I said them religiously every morning, and I repeated them out loud each evening.

You can even write your "I am" statements on a piece of paper and put them by your bed, so that when you wake up, you can read them word for word. I put my statements in another room, so that I had to get up, go to that room, and read them out loud before starting my day.

I wanted to read those "I am" statements as quickly as I could, because I was the architect. I was the one who created the affirmations, and what I wrote down was what I wanted to come true.

Now, before I go to sleep, I close my eyes and think about my "I am" statements. I want them at that exact moment, because whatever I put into my head right before I go to sleep is what my brain is going to do while I'm sleeping.

We know that the brain does not shut off, and we know that there are dreams — both good and bad. There are lots of opportunities for the brain to help us build beneficial neural pathways while we sleep, and these can help us during our waking moments.

One of my early "I am" statements was, "I am a proud parent." When I wrote this statement, I had never been a parent. My partner, Tim, and I had been together for about 15 years, and we had thought about adoption, but had never taken the next steps. So, I started repeating the statement, "I am a proud parent."

Within 30 days, I had taken in two exchange students — one from Sweden and one from Germany. It just happened out of the blue. I saw an advertisement on Facebook, and I clicked on the ad. I filled out a form, and a representative called. I interviewed, and the company sent its people to our house to make sure everything was safe and sound.

The next thing I knew, the students were flying over from their home countries. We hosted them for 10 months. Suddenly, I was a proud parent. It blew my mind.

We continue to help young people this way year after year, and now I can say that I am a proud parent of nine outstanding exchange students. They're all around the world. We visit them, call them, and talk to them, and they have become our kids. It's all because of the "I am" statement.

"I am" statements also helped me with public speaking. Even though I disliked public speaking, I knew it was necessary. I knew that I should be a good public speaker to be a good business coach. I needed to influence and inspire people. I needed to get out of the space of fear.

One of our mechanisms is teaching, and it encourages clients to enroll. So, "I am a great public speaker" became another of my first "I am" statements. I said it over and over again, and within six months of being a business coach, I found myself asking to speak at conferences.

Soon, people were asking me to speak at events, and I gave a presentation on my success thus far in ActionCOACH™. I had become a rising star among the other business coaches, because I was an excellent public speaker.

These days, I have a new set of "I am" statements. For example, one is about being a dynamic public speaker and receiving rave reviews.

Of the 20 "I am" statements on the first list that I ever wrote, two were expendable after 30 days. One of those "I am" statements was, "I am a watch collector."

Once I started repeating that affirmation, I began to look at watches. I would walk through the mall and admire the watches. In this way, my "I am" statement had led me to look at watches. It was working.

However, I didn't enjoy being a watch collector. Knowing I could control what I put on my list, I removed that "I am" statement.

Another affirmation that I removed was, "I am the proud owner of a six-seat airplane." I'm a private pilot, and I love to fly. When I started my affirmations, I thought buying an airplane of my own would be a good idea.

Thirty days later, I realized that I did not want an airplane. I removed that one and replaced it with "I am a proud owner of a BMW 7 Series."

So, I took those "I am" statements off the list and replaced them with others. Meanwhile, the other 18 affirmations came true. One was, "I am the number-one business coach in the world." Within four years of saying that "I am" statement, I became the number-one business coach in the world. Another one was, "I am free of debt, including my mortgage." At the time, I didn't know that having a mortgage was a good thing, but I learned that lesson.

Some years afterward, I was free of debt and had no mortgage. Later, I learned about how to leverage mortgages, so I am no longer debt free, because I have a mortgage and keep it as a tool for leverage. Regardless, there was a point at which my statement came true.

All the statements have come true, and now I put new ones on the list all the time. "I am the proud owner of a BMW" came true. "I am a proud owner of a Tesla" came true, too, and I now own a couple of Teslas.

"I am an international public speaker who speaks at corporate conferences" was an affirmation that I wrote in the first year of using "I am" statements. I took off "I am a great public speaker" and replaced it with "I am an international public speaker who speaks at global conferences," and since then, people have asked me to speak at events around the world.

It works, but there are rules to the use of "I am" statements that I'm going to teach you. Remember how people told me not to become an entrepreneur, and then I became one? The first rule follows the same concept. "I am" statements won't work if you say them, but let your brain think they will never happen.

Let's say your affirmation is "I am a multimillionaire." You say, "I'm a multimillionaire," but your brain's immediate response is to say that will never happen. You look around at the challenges you're facing as a business owner, and you think you'll never be a multimillionaire.

If that's your response immediately after you say your affirmation, you need to change it. Otherwise, you will build an adverse neural pathway. You will create a road that says you will never be a multimillionaire. You effectively will be deciding that you always will have problems or that you will have trouble for the rest of your life.

One of my early thought coaches taught me that "I am" statements can be helpful, but they can also be harmful.

The brain does not judge what you put into it. What you think about is what will, in turn, become the neural pathway.

Therefore, you must build the roads with a positive "I am" statement, and you must be an architect who can build upon these statements with helpful thoughts in the subsequent moments. If you happen to have a negative thought after saying an "I am" statement, supplement it with something else.

Let's go back to the statement, "I am a multimillionaire." If you say, "I am a multimillionaire," but you have a negative thought afterward, recognize the need to change and update the whole string of thoughts.

Say, "I am a multimillionaire, so I can provide more charitable donations." If your brain likes that idea and no negative thoughts arise afterward, you have successfully updated your "I am" statement to be "I am a multimillionaire, so I can provide more charitable donations."

If you continue down a negative path afterward, keep thinking of ways to update your statement so that it will end on a positive note. With "I am" statements, make sure that you are, indeed, creating affirmations that help you.

Next, limit bad architects. They are everywhere — the politics, the rhetoric, the negativity, and the finger-pointing. These are bad architects for us, and they are not helpful. We must limit who we listen to and where we focus our attention. Eliminate as many bad architects as possible.

I once had to remove a friend from my life, because that friend had become a negative architect. Everything that friend said ended on a sour note. The friend spoke poorly about everyone and everything, and it made me feel horrible. I started spending less and less time with that friend until I had set the whole friendship aside and moved on with my life. I haven't seen that person in many years. While I wish the person well, I am better off for having left the friendship in the past. In the same way, you should limit bad architects in your life, even if those people are as close as friends and family members.

Third, think about the people you want to imitate. Find their audiobooks, videotapes, and books. I wanted to imitate Brad Sugars and Jim Roone. I wanted to follow in the footsteps of successful, powerful public speakers. So, I began using those people as my architects.

Next, learn to catch yourself when you have negative thoughts. It's okay to have them; everyone does. Again, when someone cuts you off on the freeway, you may have an unfavorable reaction. Catch yourself and replace the thought with a compassionate one. Say, "I bet that person is having a bad day."

Do that over and over again, and you will create new neural pathways. Remember that we want to achieve more, because we want to give more.

ActionCOACH™ is all about world abundance through business re-education. Mindset is a skill. Work on this skill and improve your mindset, and you can achieve more. Hopefully, with the skills you have learned so far and will learn throughout the rest of this book, you can achieve more and give more.

WHAT NOW? ACTION STEPS.

- ❑ Who in your life inspired you or is one of your biggest contributors? List eight-10 of their qualities on which you plan to work harder to become a great contributor.
- ❑ Describe three examples of how you see success through your failures.
- ❑ Where in your business do you need to think bigger?
- ❑ List 10 ways you could apply the quote 'take what you need and leave the rest' to aid your journey to building your success.
- ❑ Are you currently working your business as the business owner or the owner of a job? If you answered owner of a job, describe what comes to mind thus far that you could put into action to achieve the status of business owner.
- ❑ Are there any ways that 'history is repeating' itself in your business or your life? Explain.
- ❑ In terms of skillset or mindset, how do you see your mindset? Is it thriving or taking a dive into the dark side with perfection or self-limiting beliefs?
- ❑ What are your 20 "I am" statements? Write them and begin saying them as prescribed. *Remember to modify them if after saying them aloud a couple of times, you find they do not feel like a fit.

CHAPTER 2:

WHY BOTHER?

Your reason for owning, running, and making the company great is — or will become — the fuel or the anchor to your success.

The business needs a real purpose in order for it to grow and become successful. Now, before we get too far into the discussion of purpose, let's talk a bit about the word "successful."

Achieving Your Goal (and Success)

One definition of success might be the condition of having a desirable or favorable outcome. Who decides what is desirable or favorable? Well, from a shortsighted, short-term approach, it would be the business owner or owners. When a business owner bases success only on his or her needs, a business will only achieve success slightly above the requirement to pay bills. When looking at a shortsighted, long-term approach, we see that a desirable outcome might be for the business to operate at a level that supplies a good income to the owner and the team members. Then, when looking at the business from the market perspective and long-term, we see that a desirable outcome is to be as large as possible, given the opportunity the market provides.

Here is a simple example. A dentist operates a practice. She is the only employee, and the business does well. She maximizes the business size and bases the practice's success on her willingness to work a certain number of hours. However, she can't exceed a fixed number of hours in a given week. In this case, the owner is shortsighted, meaning she is not letting the market drive her decision, and the goals are short-term, because they last only during her lifetime. She earns between $150,000 and $500,000 per year.

On the other hand, a second dentist who wants to have better success than the first would employ other dentists and allow them to take long vacations. She would pay them a sufficient income that would pay their bills and enable them to thrive. She and the employees would be able to give to charities, and together, they would work hard to build a self-sustaining business. In this case, the owner might make a few million dollars per year and have many perks that allow her to work less as a dentist and more as a business owner.

Finally, a dentist who wants to deliver a comprehensive solution to an entire market may decide to provide an excellent service and a low-cost solution to a whole city. In this case, the answer would involve owning many practice locations, having dozens of team members, and viewing the business's purpose in a broader way than anyone else in the company. In this last example, the owner sees her business's success as delivering a solution — one that she believes is beneficial — to an entire market.

Something for you to do now is to create your purpose. It should be your reason for doing what it is you're currently doing, or what you will be doing. I promise you won't find your purpose; you'll create it. Sometimes you'll create it based on what others have done. Sometimes you'll read a book, such as Simon Sinik's *Start with Why*, and it will help you create your purpose. Sometimes, you will come up with your purpose today, and then in the future, you will create a different one.

This step is a critical part of building and growing a business. What is your *why*? If you don't have one, you'll limit the size of your business, the success of your business, and the joy your business brings you and everyone else. The same will be true for team members and your customers. When the customers, the team, and the owners all understand the purpose of the business, amazing things happen.

President John F. Kennedy saw a triumphant voyage to the Moon as an element of success. He voiced that opinion in a famous speech that he delivered on September 12, 1962, at Rice Stadium in Houston, Texas.

"We choose to go to the Moon in this decade and do the other things, not because they are easy, but because they are hard, because that goal will serve to organize and measure the best of our energies and skills, because that challenge is one that we are willing to accept, one we are unwilling to postpone—."

Kennedy's vision came true on July 20, 1969, not even seven years after he gave his speech. In this way, Kennedy made the goal clear, and people came together and manifested it.

Ultimately, the definition of success comes from the company's vision. Where would the company be in 100 years if it did most things correctly, learned from mistakes, and improved over time?

Fuel. When there is fuel, fire burns well. When fuel is insufficient, fire burns out. The same is true with an engine or a body. With fuel, the engine works well, and the body thrives. Without it, the engine slows down, and the body struggles. The same goes for every business. The fuel within a business is the attitude, motivation, and spirit of the company. Many authors write about the ability of a great leader to enroll and energize teams; this ability is the fuel.

Having lived and worked in the age of Enron's rise and fall, I read much about how the company's leader, Kenneth Lay, was instrumental in the positive feelings that employees had at the company even during its darkest hour. Mr. Lay was good at keeping spirits high, which was his primary job. The full story is worth researching to help you understand the extreme highs and lows of a top Fortune 5 Company.

A company with a positive corporate culture has in place the workings of a great engine, which helps the engine operate at full strength when fuel is present. When a company is without a positive corporate culture or has a bad corporate culture, it signifies that the leader is not working to engage and inspire the team. Thus, the leader is wasting the fuel, or at a minimum, not using the fuel in the right way. It is like adding fuel to a Formula 1 race car in which only four cylinders are working in the six-cylinder engine.

Anchor. Anchors appear in business whenever there is not a specific reason for a company to succeed and prosper. When a business owner bases the success of a growing business only upon his or her needs, this condition becomes an anchor, because the company will stop growing as soon as the owner pays bills. The anchor of growing a business only to meet the needs of the current staff means that when the team becomes too busy, the business will slow down to meet the needs of the team rather than the growing demand.

Self-limiting beliefs are anchors and prevent a company from achieving greatness. Common self-limiting beliefs include ideas about hiring the right staff, working through a bad economy, expecting the market to drop someday, wondering about a hypothetical natural disaster, and worrying about the need to pay more taxes if the business performs well. That last one is a favorite of mine. I always find it amusing.

One of the biggest reasons people don't have goals is the fear of failure. Many people view failure as something negative. So many people fear failure that I thought I should include some of my thoughts on the subject of fear itself.

Face Them or Don't

Fear is a feeling we all have, because we are human. I'm not sure what creatures don't have fears. (Maybe mosquitos don't.) As far as I know, most animals have fears. Even the lion, the King of the Jungle, fears larger animals like elephants and hippopotamuses.

As cave dwellers many hundreds of thousands of years ago, humans had a lot about which to worry. Today, as humans living in a semi-civilized world, we don't have as much to fear.

If you live in a well-developed country, you hopefully do not have to worry about daily death or destruction. You hopefully do not have to worry about having food or shelter, because you have most everything you need according to Abraham Maslow's hierarchy of needs theory.

When we have a fear that we don't face, it begins to change our behaviors. We modify our behavior based on fears. Have you ever thought about it that way? It is true. Think about it.

When you see an accident on the road, you drive slowly and take a look just like everyone else does, and then you speed up and go on your way. Ever wonder why you do the same thing as everyone else? Did we ever gain great benefits or knowledge from peeking into someone else's misfortune? I never have. You probably haven't either. Why do we do it, then?

The reason is that we have a natural self-preservation mechanism. We are investigating the problem. Is there a fire? Could the problem hurt me? Is the situation so bad that I need to run away in the opposite direction? The self-preservation mechanism worked well for thousands of years, but in today's modern world, it is less useful on a day-to-day basis. Yes, we are human, and we have fears that sometimes require our attention. However, fears we've created are fears we can and should eliminate.

As I mentioned earlier in this book, some psychologists believe a person has three natural fears at birth and creates all other fears during his or her lifetime. These three fears are loud noises, falling, and abandonment. We fear loud noises that startle us, because those noises might originate from things that cause us pain.

Falling is scary, because babies need an adult to hold them safely without dropping them. Falling and hitting the ground would probably hurt. Abandonment is a natural fear, because we need adults to care for us when we are young and can't fend for ourselves.

Fears we create include the fear of public speaking, the fear of flying, the fear of insects, the fear of drowning or swimming, the fear of strangers, the fear of blood or needles, the fear of tight spaces, the fear of darkness, and another super scary one, the fear of monsters and zombies. These are all fears we manufacture, usually during our youth and often with help from friends, family, television shows, and the environment.

I once had a client who had an irrational fear of terrorists taking over the city of Houston. I didn't know the intensity of his fear until one day, during a coaching session, I learned that his fear had prevented him from doing the work that I had assigned him the previous week.

The client hadn't done any of the tasks, which would have taken him five minutes to complete, so I asked him what was preventing him from doing his work. He avoided my question, so his wife, who had joined us for the day, said, "Doug, my husband spent the last week buying guns and ammunition, because he is sure terrorists are coming to Houston!"

That comment got the client talking. I quickly learned that my client believed Houston would be attacked and taken over by a terrorist group and that it would happen soon.

Carrying around the negativity that exists in the world won't help people live a more prosperous life, and rarely will negative news help businesses improve, so I tell many clients to control their environment and their team's environment. This client and I already had talked about ways that negative news reports work against people and add to unhelpful fears. He had agreed not to watch the news or read newspapers, and he had decided to control his environment. Furthermore, this husband and wife had been clients of mine for at least six months, so I wasn't sure where the husband was finding this news about terrorists taking over Houston.

"Where did you hear about this problem?" I asked.

"Facebook," my client admitted.

"Ah, okay. It must be real, then," I said, jokingly. I smiled and chuckled.

My client got the joke, stopped defending his position, and began laughing. He realized how silly he had been. He had bought a dozen new guns, thousands of dollars of ammunition, and even built a shelter in his home — all because an idea on social media consumed his thoughts.

As my client began to realize the absurdity of the situation, I helped him remember how safe he is and how irrational his fear was. I reminded him that millions of men and women dedicate their lives to protecting people and that the military works tirelessly to combat terrorists.

After a while, my client agreed to stop paying attention to Facebook. He decided to refocus his attention back on the growth of his business. He realized that fear had taken a week — 168 hours — of his life, and he understood that, at a minimum, fear had temporarily upset his wife and his daughter as well.

What fears do you have that have limited your success? Mine are the fear of public speaking, fear of heights, fear of drowning, and fear of abandonment.

Remember the story about the skit at my training? I played the cat, because of my unwillingness to have speaking roles. It stemmed from my fear of public speaking. It took work to overcome that fear, and the work began with awareness. Frequently, we are in denial about having fears, so we need someone else to point them out. For a long time, I did not pay attention to my fears.

Now, helping people identify their fears is a daily task of mine. Once people are aware of the fear, they can see it might limit their success, so they decide to remove it.

Facing the Fear of Heights

My fear of heights still exists to this day, but I never let it stop me from learning to fly airplanes when I was 21 years old. I've walked and jumped on those glass floors in supertall buildings. I've consciously walked to the edge of buildings, indoors and outdoors, and peered over the edge. I know I won't fall, so I don't let the fear control me anymore. It is amusing to do these things, and it is okay to be afraid. I'm just not letting the fear stop me; instead, I control it.

Facing the Fear of Drowning

My fear of drowning began when I was two years old. I was walking too close to the edge of a relative's pool and fell in while people were looking the other way. I don't remember anything before being at the bottom, but my first memory of life was seeing people swim down to save me.

From then on, my parents kept me away from pools and large bodies of water. It was a precautionary response, but it was extreme. Once, I went to the lake with my family, but I didn't swim. My cousins swam. They jumped off tree limbs into the water and swung from ropes and flipped into the lake. I didn't even watch them. Instead, I sat at the tent doing something boring — not swimming or hanging out with the other kids.

That happened every summer that my grandma and grandpa took me to the lake. They loved me and wanted me to have fun, but they wouldn't allow me anywhere near the water's edge. For a while, I allowed their input to shape my opinions about the water. However, I eventually decided enough was enough.

So, I combatted my fear of drowning, and a SCUBA diver I became. I had to fight hard. I failed three times, but eventually passed the SCUBA certification class at the local YMCA. Some parts of the class were easy for me to pass. For example, I quickly passed the book lessons and tests. The swimming tests, on the other hand, were extremely difficult for me.

"Take your time. There is no time limit," the instructor said. "Swim nine laps around the pool without grabbing the edge. You can go fast or slow. You can stop and tread water. You can even float. We can be here all night."

I failed.

"Okay, come back in a couple of days and try again," the instructor said. "You've passed everything else."

I came back for another attempt.

"Just be calm," I kept telling myself as I floated and gently breathed. Before the timer went off, I almost drowned trying to get to the edge of the pool. Again, I failed.

At lunchtime on the day of my third and final attempt, I went home and practiced swimming in my pool. I measured out 19 laps (the equivalent test distance), and I wouldn't go back to work until I swam that distance without grabbing the edge of the pool.

I managed to do it at home, and when I went back to the YMCA pool, I had a newfound confidence. I managed to swim the laps, and I passed.

Nevertheless, to this day, when I jump in the water to SCUBA dive, I have a small panic attack. My heart beats rapidly, and my mind races, thinking about how much air is in my tank. I need to be the first in the water so that within the five or so minutes that everyone else gets in, I have time to settle my nerves.

It is a weird fear, and I keep working on it. I am much more comfortable going into the pool and swimming back and forth. I can go underwater (with or without SCUBA gear) with confidence and float without fear whenever I want.

Still, in those initial moments, fearful thoughts creep in, and I must remind myself to be calm. I soon relax enough to enjoy the experience, but it takes a conscious effort to face the fear. The alternative — not facing the fear — would have prevented me from SCUBA diving, which is such a positive aspect of my life.

Facing the Fear of Abandonment

One of the most personal fears I've ever faced was the fear of abandonment. I didn't even know I had this fear when I started working with ActionCOACH™.

When I eventually came to terms with having this fear, it took years of emotional examination and therapy to work through it. Facing this fear was like getting punched in the face or stabbed in the shoulder repeatedly.

87

I grew up in a challenged home. My parents endured pretty difficult childhoods themselves. My dad grew up in an orphanage, and my mom had an abusive father. Neither of my parents completed school beyond the 10th grade, and they worked low-wage, blue-collar jobs for years.

Although my parents' lives already were complicated, they added four children to the mix and had to work hard to put food on the table and a roof over our heads. Looking back, I see that they did a decent job of providing our basic needs.

Then, in my teenage years, my parents had a terrible argument, and my mom left in the middle of the night. Afterward, we didn't hear from her — or even know she was alive — for years. Eventually, we learned she had moved in with our grandma, her mom. Then, she moved in with a boyfriend of hers.

Abandonment was a word that I couldn't even say in 2009. I had suppressed those feelings to the point where I knew I was working through a complex fear that carried many emotions, but the name of that fear always evaded me.

For a couple of years, my coaches and I worked on this fear. It was a significant hurdle to overcome, because as a business coach, I sometimes lost clients. I felt the emotions of abandonment every time a client quit.

It took time to learn that clients leave for a wide range of reasons. Some people, for example, don't like to receive coaching, and that's okay. For other people, the pain of denial and regret are less painful than the pain of having a breakthrough and finding success. I know that now, but when I was working through my feelings of abandonment, all I recognized was pain from my mom leaving me.

I worked through this complicated emotion by using it as a tool for success. I pictured it as something I could point to and say, "Don't let that happen again." From a psychological point of view, that might not have been a great approach, but it worked well from a business standpoint.

I began to work harder to make sure clients stayed. When they did leave, I reminded myself that it was their decision, not mine.

My dad passed away many years ago, and I never considered his death as abandonment. It's strange how that aspect of the story worked itself out in my mind, but I never resented him for passing away.

Plus, I eventually worked through many of the issues that stood in the way of my relationship with my mom. Today, we have a healthy relationship and I enjoy our time together. In the end, I found a method of using fear to my advantage as fuel instead of an anchor. I can't advise whether doing so would be good or bad for anyone else. It just is what it is, and it has helped me in my life.

Because I faced the fear of open water and learned to SCUBA dive, I now see parts of the world many other people cannot. Because I faced the fear of public speaking, I now speak in front of large audiences and influence thousands of business leaders. Writing this book, which people around the world can read, is a way of facing the fear of rejection and ridicule. All these changes have been positive in my life. They began with the awareness of a fear. Then, I consciously decided to learn from the fears and eliminate them as best as possible.

Perhaps the moral here is that everyone has fears to face. Figure out what your fears are and face them in healthy ways. Never let fear control you. Instead, work to become aware of the fear. Embrace it. Learn about it. Then tackle it and eliminate it from your life. It won't be easy, but remain vigilant and fight through the difficult emotions that arise along the way. I promise that it will be worth it in the end. Life is too short to live in fear.

Company Vision

Creating a corporate vision may seem like a challenging task. However, I'm going to help you make it as easy as possible. Remember, the purpose of a vision is to enroll and inspire all the stakeholders, team members, customers, vendors, and business owners. Everyone needs inspiration to do the challenging tasks that are necessary for a company to become successful.

Step 1. Create a long-term, multi-generational goal. Think decades out into the future, perhaps beyond your life and your kids' and grandkids' lives. This goal is one that might make skeptics laugh. Some people might tell you that it is impossible and unrealistic. That's when you know you have a worthwhile and long-term vision.

Here are some vision statements that you might remember. Think of how these statements would enroll and inspire the team, the customers, the vendors, and the company leaders:

- We will eradicate polio.
- We will help people live longer, healthier, happier lives.
- We will put a computer on every desk in every home.
- We will offer the world's best quick-service restaurant experience.
- We will use the power of Moore's Law to bring smart, connected devices to every person on Earth.
- We will become the world's most-loved, most-flown, and most-profitable airline.
- We will fulfill people's dreams through the experience of motorcycling.
- We will be the world's most customer-centric company.
- We will become the world's leading consumer company for automotive products and services.
- We will accelerate the advent of sustainable transport by bringing mass-market electric cars to the market as soon as possible.
- We will establish our coffee company as the most-recognized and most-respected brand in the world.

- We will be the Harvard of the West Coast.
- We will develop leaders who one day will make a global difference.
- We will make people happy.
- We will be the most comprehensive entertainment company in the world.
- We will satisfy all our customers' financial needs.
- We will become the world leader in connecting people to wildlife and conservation.

Some of these vision statements have developed and evolved, helping the companies redefine their goals over the years. Don't worry about making the perfect vision statement. Start with what first comes to mind. Then, change and improve it as time goes by. The vision for my coaching business is, "Each week, we will help 1,800 businesses reach their success and exceed their dreams."

The ActionCOACH™ vision statement is to create "world abundance through business re-education." That goal is deep and long-term. World abundance means no one is starving. It means everyone has a shelter. It means people are comfortable and able to support their families. Through business re-education, abundance becomes possible. When a business owner provides for his or her family and team members for multiple generations, new possibilities arise, and people can contribute to organizations and charities that help world abundance happen.

No one can take their fortunes with them after death. Once a business owner's heirs are comfortable, it is time for the business owner to help people that he or she doesn't know. For example, you might think about helping people in your community, helping people hundreds of miles away, or helping people in deprived locations. All these things are possible when a business is super successful.

The ActionCOACH™ vision is one that enrolls and inspires the leaders, franchise partners, partners, team members, clients, and clients' employees. Believing in world abundance through business re-education is a significant reason I continue to help business owners.

Here are some examples of industry-specific vision statements that companies now use, and with minor modifications, could become yours.

A furniture company: "Provide the most comfortable, most accessible furniture at the best possible price to everyone in the world."

A restaurant company: "Help every person on the planet have food equal or better to what we serve here, because of our success and ability to give to others who are less fortunate."

An IT services company: "Eliminate the ability of viruses to infiltrate any of our clients."

A coaching company: "Become an organization that helps 1,800 business owners every week and creates solutions for senior team members."

WHAT NOW? ACTION STEPS.

- ❑ What are your top five fears about the future of your business as it relates to your personal goals for your life?
- ❑ Write about how you are using fear. Is it acting as fuel or an anchor?
- ❑ How is your vision for your business creating purpose for those in your sphere? Like your employees, family, vendors, and your other personal relationships.
- ❑ What is your vision for your business and personal life?

CHAPTER 3:

THE SECRET

Some people know the secret. Others think they know it. You and I can tell those people apart. It is the difference between successful companies and not-so-successful companies. First, let's be clear what marketing is and what it is not. Marketing is a practice to generate leads for a business. It is not a practice of getting clients or having the sales team drum up leads and close them with some magic pill. Marketing is a business component to get someone to say, "I'm interested in what you are selling."

Way too many companies combine marketing and sales into one role. It is a huge mistake. The skills and behaviors necessary to be a good marketer are different from those necessary to be a great salesperson. They can't be more different. They are night and day.

I didn't learn this until I was in my early 40s. I already had built and sold a couple of companies, yet I didn't understand marketing. This information is a testament to the five-legged stool concept. You can be good at three of the Five Pillars and still have a decent company. Having five of the Five Pillars makes it exhilarating to own a business.

Story: I've always had a fascination with cool cars, perhaps because of my childhood in the Detroit area, which, of course, has a rich history in the automobile manufacturing industry. Some years ago, I went to one of the major auto shows that tours the United States each year.

At the Ford Motor Car display, I saw the new Ford Fusion. It was a nice car, and it was a new model, and it even had a hybrid option — half electric and half combustion. The presentation was neat, and the presenters made a tempting offer. They handed out free T-shirts that were attractive and read "Ford Fusion." The presenters said that my friends and I could receive a $50 Visa gift card if they wore the T-shirt around the auto show. I thought it a pretty good deal.

They said we also had to know the estimated mileage of the Ford Fusion, because people would approach us and ask. I thought that was a good deal, too. A third catch was that people could only activate the gift card by visiting a Ford dealership. It was still a great offer, so my friends and I quickly grabbed T-shirts, tossed them on, and wore them around the showroom.

As we walked around, people did approach us and asked about the estimated miles per gallon for the Ford Fusion. We knew the answer was 42 miles per gallon, so we told them. We were correct, so the people congratulated us and said we had all won $50 Visa gift cards. That was fun.

Do you think Ford knows how many $50 Visa gift cards it gives out on average at every show? Yes, it knows. Do you think it knows how many of those cards people activate at a dealership? Again, yes, it certainly does. Do you think Ford knows the average number of cards that people activate compared to the number of cars people buy, because of this marketing strategy? There's no question. The company knows. Most likely, Ford makes a good return on its investment with this strategy.

Let's do some quick math to understand this marketing method.

If Ford gives away 500 T-shirts that cost $2 each and an equal number of Visa gift cards that cost nothing at first, Ford pays $1,000.

Let's say half of the people activate their gift cards at a dealership. That means 250 people have $50 gift cards, so Ford pays $12,500.

That means Ford invests $13,500 to get 250 people to visit their dealership showrooms. Although test driving a car was not a requirement of the strategy, many of those 250 probably will while they are at the dealership.

Let's say the Gross Profit of selling a new car is $15,000. That number is much greater than $13,500, and the company only needs to sell one car to break-even or make a profit.

If Ford only makes two sales out of 250 prospective customers, the strategy would still have a positive ROI even though the number conversion rate would be a dismal eight-tenths of 1%. (i.e., 2 sales ÷ 250 prospective customers = .008 conversions).

That amount is less than one out of 100. Nevertheless, the company wins.

Plus, if the car is great — and I can attest that the Ford Fusion was great, because I bought one that year — the company might gain a repeat customer.

So, now you know that math is one major piece of the marketing secret. We'll examine that topic in more detail soon.

The full secret is that a successful business is excellent at marketing. That's it. it's just marketing. Marketing is the secret.

Think of the busy businesses out there. Think of the world's largest companies. The world's largest restaurant, McDonald's, is doggone good at marketing, especially to kids, who often have a significant influence on where a family will eat.

In Houston, there is a super successful furniture company called Gallery Furniture. It is one of the largest independent furniture stores in the country. The founder failed at all kinds of strategies some 35 years ago. Then he found one that worked. He began to run low-budget, late-night television commercials that ended with the saying, "Gallery Furniture really will save you money!" He did that over and over again. The marketing worked, and he discovered the secret to having a mega-business.

We'll continue to look at this secret in more detail.

Question: On a scale from one to 10 with 10 being high, what is your confidence level with your marketing skills?

Activity: If you would rank your confidence level at an eight or nine, take a detailed analysis of your marketing strategies over the past year. Invest a couple of hours thoroughly considering what worked, what worked well, what worked moderately, and what didn't work at all. What secret did you discover?

If you would rank your confidence level at a seven or below, continue educating yourself on marketing. Buy as many marketing books as possible, and look for books by marketing experts, such as Seth Godin and Brad Sugars. You must become a great marketer to have a very successful business.

Let's move on to some specific tasks for the marketing of your business.

Your Unique Selling Position

Your company's Unique Selling Position (USP) is an essential piece of the business. The most important part of the USP is what is "unique" about your company. Having something that stands out is critical.

Here is an example that I think will help everyone understand what happens with and without a good USP. Many decades ago, gas stations were just gas stations — places to go to fill a car up with gasoline. They all did the same thing. They all pumped your gas.

Each gas station charged about the same amount per gallon (or liter) of gasoline. It was a profitable business with good margins. The only things that might stand out between one gas station and another were the location and perhaps the friendliness of the attendants.

Everything changed in the 1980s. One after another, gas stations added convenience stores to their business models. Initially, the uniqueness of seeing a gas station as a place where a person could also get groceries was a great feature. It made these gas stations different and something special to see and visit. People chose these gas stations without giving much concern to the gas prices.

Eventually, however, most gas stations had a convenience store. The uniqueness disappeared. Over the years, petroleum companies kept coming up with one uniqueness after another. Each time, it was unique for a while, and then everyone else did the same thing.

For example, they tried selling "special additives" to enhance the combustion, clean the carburetor, improve the mileage — and maybe make your car happy. They added car washes, 24-hour stores, hot dog carts, and ice cream machines. Whatever one gas station added, another quickly adopted.

Remember, when there was a unique element to the business, the people who chose to visit specialty gas stations did not have much concern about the gas prices. This phenomenon happens in every industry. When a business offers uniqueness, customers have fewer sensitivities about price, and the company can sell things at higher prices. On the other hand, a business can compete only on price when there is no uniqueness or when the thing that the business thinks is unique turns out to be something that everyone can claim or emulate, such as good customer service.

Today, many gas stations have found an excellent uniqueness. They now connect their stores to branded food chains. Although the gas stations each follow the same concept, the uniqueness is that each fast food chain is different from one gas station to the next.

For example, you can enjoy a McDonald's hamburger after you get your gas and groceries from the Exxon on Main Street, or you can fill up your car's tank, buy groceries, and visit Starbucks at the BP on First Street. If kids are in the car and want a McDonald's happy meal, you might go to Exxon, eat at McDonald's, and pick up groceries in the store. If you are on your way to work in the morning, you might fill up on gas at BP, get a coffee at Starbucks, and buy a snack for lunch in the store. Either way, you won't pay much attention to gas prices, because you'll only be thinking about the USP.

As you can see, it can be challenging to stay on top with uniqueness, even for trillion-dollar enterprises. It took petroleum companies decades to create something that might stick. Even then, they probably know that USP is always replaceable. It can adapt and change. You must update your USP whenever your competitors duplicate what you're already doing.

Here are some USPs that your competitors cannot duplicate.

1) Your USP could be about your life. This one is compelling to prospective customers, and it is all yours. Nobody has the same story as you. Restaurants sometimes put their story on their menu somewhere. Every time their USP is interesting to read. People like to hear about the journey.

2) Think of what frustrates your customers or makes them nervous about dealing with your industry. Maybe they fear that a business will take advantage of them. These are stereotypical fears people have about used car dealers. Nowadays, some used car dealers offer buying experiences without haggling. In doing so, they resolve customers' anxiety and frustration. This resolution is now the uniqueness of the business. When you think about the frustrations that occur in your industry, you can take a leading USP approach toward marketing.

Activity: List five USPs. Write them down and try not to limit or edit your ideas. Brainstorm USPs that would be good to have. Under each of the five USPs, list names of any other businesses in the same industry with the same USPs or similar ones. Also, list how the market would respond to your specific USP. Finally, rank your USPs in the order of how easy they would be to implement. In the end, you should have a list of USPs that you can continue to examine, develop, update, and leverage.

Your Guarantee

In business, a guarantee is one of the single most powerful tools for getting and keeping a client. It eliminates the fears that exist in making a purchase. Guarantees may range from a simple model, such as a satisfaction guarantee, to a secure model, such as a 100% money-back guarantee.

There have been industries created, because of a guarantee. For example, consider the "30-minute-or-free guarantee." In the 1980s, Domino's Pizza wanted to gain massive market share while eliminating as many of the issues with pizza delivery as possible; in this case, problems were usually pizzas arriving cold or late. The company resolved its problems with the "30-minute-or-free guarantee," which revolutionized the pizza delivery industry. The company assured customers that it would deliver pizzas within 30 minutes or else the pizza would be free.

How about the "absolutely positively has to be there overnight, guaranteed" offer? Who do you think made that one? Quite a few people might say it was UPS, because UPS now has a strong foothold in the industry, but actually Federal Express created this guarantee. Then the overnight delivery business flourished, and other companies — like UPS — joined the crowd.

Both the Domino's guarantee and the Federal Express guarantee are now history. Now that both companies have a significant portion of their respective markets, they have new guarantees.

Important: Your company should have a meaningful guarantee. Without a solid guarantee, you might be missing out on customers who are scared to buy from your industry. Every business can have a guarantee. Even businesses that follow strict regulations, such as financial businesses, can have them. Businesses can guarantee to return calls or emails within a day. If financial services can have guarantees, your businesses can as well.

What do you think of this guarantee? A behavior modification coach says, "I will not receive payment unless your peers — not I — can determine that your behavior has changed. If the behavior doesn't change, I will receive nothing." This concept is a guarantee on results.

How about this guarantee? A fitness coach says, "Choose an amount of weight that you want to lose during the program's timeframe, and if you don't lose all of it, you can get back 100% of your payments." This idea is a money-back guarantee on results. I once worked with a fitness company, and it took me a full year to convince the owners to offer this guarantee. However, they tripled their business in three months after implementing the guarantee.

Here is a guarantee I helped create for a veterinary clinic client. Working with the client, I asked about the most significant frustrations customers seemed to have with the vet industry. The answer was that customers hated waiting. In response, the clinic created a guarantee that clients could see the vet in 10 minutes, or the clinic would waive the visitation fee. Afterward, the clinic delivered on this guarantee. Clients appreciated it, and the clinic gained repeat business.

Here is one more guarantee. A business coach guarantees that every dollar a client invests must return to the business's bottom line within 17 weeks of that client starting the program. Otherwise, the coaching continues for free until there is at least a dollar-for-dollar ROI.

Important: Remember, a guarantee is a marketing tool. Expect to pay, because of the guarantee from time to time, but understand that any payment you make is, in the end, a marketing cost.

Exercise: Determine what would be excellent and novel guarantees for your industry. Write three of them down. Determine how it would be possible to deliver on these guarantees. Some cases might depend on the customer doing something or agreeing to something for the guarantee to be valid.

Once you have decided on your guarantees, be sure you can deliver on them as often as possible. Finally, advertise your guarantees anywhere your prospective customers might see — on a website, inside sales material, on your business cards, and so on. This concept has significant merit, because of something called "what's in it for me" (WIIFM), which is a factor that will significantly increase your company's ability to earn customers.

A Company 10x10

When creating a marketing campaign and an overall marketing plan, make sure your business has options from which to pick and implement. I created a 10x10 matrix that allows you to evaluate up to 100 marketing strategies and see what might work for your business. Yes, I "might" is a keyword of that last sentence. The reality is most marketing doesn't work, but when you figure out what marketing does work, you are well on your way to having a super successful company.

Gallery Furniture, which I mentioned previously, tried plenty of marketing strategies. Nothing worked for a long time, and then, something did. That one strategy has been the company's go-to strategy for more than 30 years. They have a USP, and they have a guarantee. They also have quite a few marketing plans in place, and they use them month after month.

Here is how a 10x10 marketing strategy matrix works. First, come up with 10 categories of marketing strategies. Here are several that are appropriate for many industries:

- Direct Mail
- Internet
- Networking
- Speaking
- Trade Shows

Use any of these that might work well for your business or in your industry. Under each of these categories, come up with 10 ways to execute a specific strategy within that category.

For example, you might write that your business can go to a national trade show for your industry under the Trade Shows category. That would be a great way to implement a specific strategy within that category. You could attend a trade show for your industry specifically, or a sector that needs the product you are selling.

Picture a technology company that sells customer relationship management (CRM) systems. The company could attend trade shows specifically about CRMs, but it also could show up at retail trade shows, restaurant trade shows, medical practice trade shows, and so on. For your business, research the 10 options for this specific category of strategies, and find opportunities to engage.

Exercise: Download the 10x10 Marketing Plan sample from our shared website, www.thefivePillarsbook.com/downloads. Edit the spreadsheet to match your industry. Keep the categories and rows that match your industry. Delete the other categories and strategies, and then replace them with your own categories and strategies.

On an ongoing basis, track the numerical results from each campaign. There are multiple tabs in the spreadsheet to track the results, the ROI, and the budget for each strategy.

Over time learn about 10 of the strategies that give the most amount of ROI in the shortest time. These will be your 10 strategies to create great successful companies.

Important: Most marketing strategies take a long time to reap any rewards of hard work. It would be unwise for an up-and-coming company to use those strategies. A start-up wants to gain customers quickly, as a large amount of money flows out of the company daily during the early weeks and months.

When I created my first 10x10 for my business-coaching practice, I worked hard and did the project justice. I thought about all the ways that a business-coaching practice could market itself by generating leads. I then created the 10x10 and focused my initial energies on a couple of the categories, specifically Networking and Speaking. I used a few strategies in each of these categories, and within four months, I had become one of the fastest start-up franchisees in the company's 15-year history. As I continued to fine-tune the strategies, I leveraged eight to 10 strategies each month, and they were all from the original 10x10 that I created. Within four years,

I became the top franchisee in the world; that's out of 1,000 coaches in 42 countries.

I learned that marketing is math, and people behind a computer screen do it best. People who understand the math behind the strategies are the most qualified people for the job. The ROI for each marketing strategy is what makes that approach worth doing over and over again.

Story: One of our clients was moderately successful when we met. This client had one location, worked long hours, and was making a good income. However, the client didn't know the numbers behind certain aspects of the company. In the first few weeks, I coached the client to work on the ROI on a few campaigns.

The good news was that the data was available. In many cases, clients do not track anything; however, this client had tracked everything. It turned out the client simply didn't analyze thoroughly.

Then, we saw something fantastic while looking at the results of a direct mail campaign two years earlier. We noticed that the direct mail campaign had paid for itself within just 45 days. The client had not repeated this direct mail campaign, because the client thought it had been a waste of money and not worth the effort of breaking even. In this case, as is often the case, the break-even point was just the beginning. Because the company received the profits from new sales quickly, it could and should have employed these campaigns frequently. Now, the client does.

The reality was that, over two years, the break-even point had become an 800% ROI. The customers kept coming back and buying more, and they referred the company to other new customers. Because of the lack of analysis, this client lost out on two years of marketing that certainly would have provided a similar ROI.

Another realization is that a marketing campaign should not break the bank. It should not be the holy grail of business growth. Businesses need to test, measure, duplicate, and magnify marketing strategies when they work. When a strategy doesn't work, the business should change it first and test it afterward. Then, if the strategy still does not support a positive ROI, the company can, at last, remove it.

A business should have eight to 12 working strategies in place. Doing so allows the continually changing markets to have processes that work, if and when some begin to fail. As that occurs, the company will see only a slight dip in the number of leads it generates while implementing new strategies.

The Measurement of Everything

Although not always a necessity, measuring is a tremendous opportunity for every business that is not public. If a business is a public company, the regulations that go along with being public mean that there are lots of measurements to report. Failing to do so if your business is a public company means you will incur significant fines and run the risk of going to jail. Private companies do not have these rules and, therefore, often do not measure much of anything besides revenue and profits. In fact, business owners of private companies frequently overlook the measurement of the revenue and profits, and instead, they focus on the cash in the bank account.

There are many things to measure. A business needs to measure leads, revenue, profits, conversion rate, number of active customers, and the average tenure of a customer. It should determine the frequency of a customer, the profit margins of each product, the time it takes to make or acquire the product, and the amount of time the product is on the shelf. Review the time it takes to send an invoice and the time it takes to get paid. Find out the revenue per day, revenue per hour, and revenue per employee. Businesses must identify the number of up-sales and the dollars of those up-sales. Plus, it should measure the number and dollars of up-sales per person. The list goes on.

Measurement is numerical. Whatever is measured must end up being a number. Measuring customer service and employee satisfaction will result in numerical data that a business will most likely get from a survey. We must be able to see all trends, including flat, declining, and increasing trends. Understanding a lead's origin — meaning which strategy brought about a lead — is fundamental for a business that wants to know where to invest its marketing funds.

Understanding which salesperson has the best conversion rate helps a business compare that number to the industry average. Here are some of the things to measure in each of the Five Pillars. Great companies measure all of this data and more.

Marketing, the First Pillar: Measure the cost to acquire a lead, the cost to acquire a customer, the conversion rate per strategy, the number of referrals by client type, break-even calculations on both days and income, the marketing budget based on company goals and viewed against the success of each month, the lifetime value of a customer, and the ROI on each marketing campaign.

Sales, the Second Pillar: Measure the company conversion rate, the average dollar sale, the average profit per sale, and track those measurements for each customer, team, shift, hour, day, week, month, quarter, and so on.

Operations, the Third Pillar: Be sure to measure the profit margins per product; the time it takes to acquire a product; the time the product is in inventory; the number of products the business produces per hour, day, week, quarter, and year; the customer satisfaction rate; the maximum utilization rate; the current utilization rate; the optimum utilization rate; and both the downtime and uptime per machine and person.

Finance, the Fourth Pillar: Measure the profits and the revenue, and track them per day, week, month, quarter, year, and so on. Measure the cost of capital; the cost of debt; the return on capital; the return on debt; the opportunity cost; the company share value — even for non-public companies; the assets; the liabilities, the long-

and short-term liabilities; the accounts receivable; the aging on receivables; the bad debt; the cash flow; and the long- and short-term cash flow forecasts.

Team, the Fifth Pillar: Measure the team satisfaction; the average cost per team member; the average revenue and average profit per team member; the team member counts; the percent of the team using all the benefits; and the cost and ROI of benefits packages.

There are another 100 measurements in the business not listed. There is a saying: If it's worth doing, it's worth measuring.

Key Performance Indicators

KPIs or Key Performance Indicators are like the dials in a car or the instruments in an airplane. You don't have to read the dials, but if you don't, you might face unpleasant consequences. A KPI is what the business sees as an essential measurement to record and track over time, improve through new strategies, and replace once irrelevant.

The most common KPI is revenue, which many people know as sales. (Some people outside of the United States call it turnover.) It is the top-line figure on an income statement, also called a Profit and Loss Statement or P&L.

In business, many terms mean the same thing. It can be confusing for a business owner or team member who hears one term and then thinks the meaning is another.

A common term I have forgotten from time to time is "gross revenue." This term means the top-line revenue. Frequently, it means the top-line revenue minus the cost of goods sold, which results in Gross Profit.

What matters most is that the business owner and his or her appropriate team members know what to measure.

Example:

Income Statement

- Revenue: $100,000
- COGS: (55,000)
- Gross Profit: $45,000
- Expenses: $20,000
- Net Profit: $25,000

I will address important KPIs in Finance, the Fourth Pillar section. Here, I will review important KPIs for marketing. Marketing KPIs for every business include:

- Leads generated
- Visitors to website
- Forms and phone calls from website
- Cost per lead
- Cost per new client
- Lifetime value of a client

Remember that marketing is all about generating leads. Therefore, one of the main KPIs within marketing is the number of leads that a business generates for the period it is measuring. This timeframe can be a month, a quarter, a year, multiple years, and even days, hours, or minutes.

How you determine the frequency depends upon the speed at which the business generates leads.

If you are tracking the number of visitors to your company's website — and you should be — you might measure by the minute, especially if your business is a large company like IBM™. Now, don't let me confuse you. A visitor to a website is probably not officially a lead. I would think of a website visitor as a lead if that person filled out a form, downloaded trackable information, sent a message, or called you, because of what they found on the website. The first KPI for marketing is the number of leads.

The next KPI for marketing is the cost per lead. Get this figure by dividing the marketing investment that the business makes during a specific time by the number of leads. You can break this KPI into all the lead sources you want to measure — and yes, you should measure all lead sources.

The cost per lead is another critical KPI to track. It will determine the quantity of the leads based on the marketing strategy you use. If you have a website company, this KPI can tell you how many people search your area for the product or service you offer. Using this data, you can find out the cost to get to a single lead. That figure is the KPI called cost per lead. It is a good practice to track the cost per lead for the company and each of the marketing strategies.

Another critical KPI to track is the company's break-even per marketing strategy. It requires some KPI information from other areas, including the Sales Pillar and the Finances Pillar.

Example:

If you own a website and have a $3,000 monthly budget for search engine optimization (SEO), and your average profit per sale is $500, your break-even will be six sales. (6 sales x $500 per sale profit = $3,000 of profit).

Therefore, the KPI would show six sales as the break-even for the website SEO strategy. You would need to revisit this KPI as the average profit per sale fluctuated according to the finance team's calculations.

Another KPI required in this area is the conversion rate. How many leads are needed, on average, to make one sale? In this example, we can say it takes four leads to get to one sale. That means that, on average, every fourth sale opportunity that occurs will result in a $500 profit.

Multiplying the four leads by the six sales shows that the business would need to process 24 leads to generate six sales and equal the $3,000 in profits necessary for break-even according to this marketing strategy.

In this example, let's say a lead costs $100. We measured our lead-to-sale Conversion Rate.

The business can get one sale for every four leads, or a 25% conversion rate. If we want six sales, we need 24 leads. If each lead costs $100, 24 leads costs $2,400.

Therefore, the business should invest $2,400 to acquire six sales. If each sale has a profit of $150, we can say 24 sales equals $3,600 in profit.

In other words, the company should invest $2,400 for $3,600 in profit. The profit due to marketing ($1,200) is the difference between the marketing investment ($2,400) and the profit ($3,600).

As soon as the business has its measurement, it quickly should reinvest. Measurement is key to marketing, and KPI management is key to business growth and success.

Activity: List your top six KPIs for your marketing management. Have the measurement mechanism in place within seven days, and within 30 days, measure your first full month. A great goal is to have all the measurement mechanisms in place to manage the Marketing Pillar KPIs within 90 days.

Important: Peter Drucker once said, "What gets measured gets improved." The line hits home for many business owners. What you are aware of becomes better. No matter what you measure, whether it's marketing, selling, generating leads, or any other important KPI, the awareness of the measurement is the key to improvement.

Once you have established the KPIs and begun to review them at least monthly, it is time to analyze the results and create strategies to improve them. Businesses frequently forget or underutilize this task, but it is a significant task that answers the fundamental question behind every report: "What does this mean?"

A Typical Work Week for the Marketing Role

People often ask me what a marketing person can do for a company. It is an excellent question that the company must answer before it hires a marketing expert, not days, weeks, or months afterward. It seems like a straightforward and logical step; however, ask around, and you'll discover that many struggling businesses fail to organize a weekly schedule of tasks to perform, KPIs to report, and results to deliver. This part of the Marketing Pillar will fix those issues for the marketing expert you hire. It could also fix those issues for other team members at the business if you follow the same process with them.

Let's first outline all the possible tasks of a marketing person in a relatively small business. Every company needs to document these tasks thoroughly and then measure them consistently to make sure the role is delivering proper value to the business. As the company grows, each of these tasks becomes more detailed and more frequent. Potentially, each project could one day become an entire job function for one person or many people to perform daily.

In this example, we'll consider the marketing coordinator for an accounting practice that is nearing one million dollars in revenue. I require my clients to have a marketing coordinator on board by the time their business reaches the million-dollar level.

The accounting practice would measure the marketing coordinator on his or her ability to generate leads, which in this case would be clients for the practice. Therefore, one of the KPIs will be the number of leads per month. The practice would see a lead as any company that requested a bid for work, or at a minimum, asked about the prices of the services.

A second KPI would be the percent of leads that converted to a client, or the conversion rate. A third would be the number of prospective customers that came to the firm either through digital or in-person means.

For this example, I will add what I call the Five-Pack to measure a website for lead generation. The Five-Pack is the number of visitors, the average time each customer spent on the website, the number of leads the website generated, the bounce rate or percent of people who left the website after visiting only one page, and the total number of minutes that the average person spent on the website.

Having determined the KPIs for the role, the business now can choose tasks for the marketing coordinator and outline a weekly schedule.

Tasks for the Marketing Coordinator	Time per Week	Days/Times in the Week
Update website blogs and other content	4 hours	Mon, Thu 2 hours per day 8:30–10:30 a.m.
Attend networking events	6 hours	Tue, Fri 3 hours per day 8:30–10 a.m. and 4:30–6 p.m.
Write content for distribution	12 hours	Mon, Tue, Wed 4 hours per day 10:30 a.m.–3:30 p.m. (1 hour for lunch)
Study industry trends	2 hours	Thu 2 hours 10:30 a.m.–12:30 p.m.
Report and review KPIs	2 hours	Fri 2 hours 2:30–4:30 p.m.
Execute strategies to achieve goals of lead generation	14 hours	Mon, Tue, Wed, Thu, Fri Mon, Tue: 3:30–5:30 p.m. Wed: 8:30–10:30 a.m. Thu: 1:30–5:30 p.m. Fri: 8:30–11:30 a.m. and 4:30–5:30 p.m.

Activity: Determine your marketing coordinator's KPIs, tasks, and daily schedule for the standard 40-hour workweek. This list of tasks should represent a typical schedule, but not an obligatory schedule for each day. At the same time, this schedule should represent what you expect the marketing coordinator to focus on during typical days when no extraneous tasks take precedence. Unless you plan for emergency time, which would not be likely in the case of an accounting firm, sticking to this schedule should be the norm.

A Challenge You Can Win

The opportunity or challenge within the Marketing Pillar is to keep the Sales Pillar busy. One of the two Pillars should be growing bigger and stronger than the other. When that happens back and forth, month after month, you will know that your business is on the road to success.

You win the challenge by creating enough leads for the sales team that the sales team cannot process them all at once. Then the Sales Pillar becomes the winning Pillar. When the sales team is not busy processing leads, the Sales Pillar is winning.

With good KPIs, useful strategies, proper action, and plenty of morale-boosting, the Marketing Pillar can be the most exciting — and frequently the most successful —

Pillar unless you are in the thick of managing the Sales Pillar.

WHAT NOW? ACTION STEPS.

- ❑ What is your WIIFM stated in your guarantee and unique selling proposition? If it is not, how can you recreate the messages to use in your marketing?
- ❑ After downloading the 10x10 marketing matrix, identify your 10 to begin your marketing plan. What are the top three from the plan that you can put into action with tracking and measuring their results?
- ❑ Which of your five Pillars are not being tracked, measured, or analyzed in your business? Choose the one that needs the most attention and create the strategies to put in place, so you can measure the effectivity.
- ❑ How are you using KPI's? Which area needs more development?
- ❑ What is your KPI management plan?
- ❑ How is your Five Pack being documented?

CHAPTER 4:

YOU PAID FOR THE LEAD.
DON'T WASTE IT.

As you've learned from the Marketing Pillar, leads are worth money. You paid a certain amount of money and time to produce the lead. Many businesses fail to understand that the lead is equal to cash, and they can either turn that cash into a positive or negative return on their investment. This Pillar ensures all the proper steps are in place and performing in ways that maximize the ROI on marketing investments.

Human Behaviors in Sales

It took me years to realize in the fullest sense that not everyone is like me, and trust me, not everyone is like you either. Having worked with thousands of business owners, I believe this realization was one of the most surprising discoveries of my professional life.

A good friend and former client of mine explained it best when he used the analogy of a foreign language. This friend also happened to be a trainer on four-quadrant behavior patterns, which are behavior assessments based on American psychologist William Moulton Marston's theories on human emotion and personality, so my friend understood the topic of human behavior well.

My friend said that if you speak only English and meet someone who speaks only Mandarin, you might be hard-pressed to have a worthwhile conversation with that person. Yes, there are many tools available to help bridge the gap. Nonetheless, it will be a difficult discussion. The funny thing is that when it comes to behaviors, the same is true.

If you are direct, to the point, impatient, outgoing, and somewhat loud, you might annoy and irritate many other people. The opposite of someone with those qualities is someone sincere, calm, patient, and relatively quiet. This person prefers to take things at a slow pace. Each of these examples is common in our world, yet few people realize how important it is to know whether they have the former or latter personality type, so that they can play to their strengths during sales conversations.

Grab a pen and a piece of paper. Take 30 seconds to write down an answer to the following question. Ready? "How was your weekend?"

Let's think about your response. Maybe you wrote something like, "It was good. I spent time with my family. I went to the park and had fun."

Perhaps you wrote a brief answer that kept to the point, such as, "It was good." Alternatively, maybe your response was like a checklist of accomplishments.

"How was your weekend?" is a simple question. But the way people answer often puts them in one of two groups, task-oriented individuals or people-oriented individuals. Task-oriented individuals are, in the four-quadrant behavior pattern world, the direct and impatient people or the outgoing and fun-loving people. People-oriented individuals are, in the four-quadrant behavior pattern world, the caretakers or the rule followers.

Frequently, the other person's answer will reveal how he or she communicates best. This information can help you decide how to approach future conversations with that person.

There is one more thing to add to this equation. Consider what you hear when the person gives his or her answer. If it seems excited or loud, the person might be a direct person or an outgoing person. If it sounds calm or muted, the person might be a caretaker or a rule follower.

Considering the other person's response, you can ascertain the person's placement on the four-quadrant behavior pattern scale. You can identify whether the person is a direct person, an outgoing person, a caretaker, or a rule follower within seconds, and then you can use this information to have a fruitful conversation.

Picture a business meeting. The leader begins by casually discussing brief details about his or her weekend and then talks briefly about something pleasant someone else at the company is experiencing. Another person in the room is wondering, "Why can't we get to the point of the meeting?" Often, situations like this one occur, because the leader of the meeting and the restless participant have opposite four-quadrant behavior pattern profiles. Thus, there is a chance of conflict between those people.

Now, reverse the profiles. The meeting's leader is always keen on getting down to business, and the participant has the opposite personality. This time, the participant wonders, "Why do we always go directly to work issues? I'm a person, not a machine. Can't we show some friendliness and warmth before we get to the numbers?"

"Communication is the response you get." That saying is one of the core skills taught at ActionCOACH™. With this understanding of communication, you need to focus on speaking in the recipient's language — in a way that targets the recipient's four-quadrant behavior pattern profile. Taking ownership of this notion is a vital realization to become a successful salesperson.

I tell my clients to record the four-quadrant behavior pattern profile they suspect each of their customers and prospective customers has. Then, I teach the team to communicate in the four-quadrant behavior pattern language. Remember, it is about the business reaching the customer, not the other way around.

Tip: Nowadays, businesses ought to have a customizable customer relationship management (CRM) system. However, if your business does not have one, use the middle-initial field of a person's name as his or her four-quadrant behavior pattern. This way, everyone becomes accustomed to the use of four-quadrant behavior pattern in daily conversations with the customer.

Important: The four-quadrant behavior pattern is a crucial element in building a successful business, and it is a hidden area or blindspot for most people.

Seven Steps or More

Jeffrey Gitomer, whom I have mentioned, explains that people love to buy, but hate when people sell to them. From ActionCOACH™, I learned that the definition of selling is professionally helping people to buy. It was a mindset shift. Helping people to buy is not selling at all. Instead, it is providing a service that helps people get what they want, not what you want to convince them to get.

There is a big difference between this concept and the way many people learn to sell. The act of selling should be a helpful, positive exchange between the salesperson and the customer. When it is, the sales should increase and the sales experience should improve for both the customer and the salesperson.

The sales process is like a dance with precise choreography. It is an emotional and logical step-by-step process, and it has definitive rules to follow with surgical precision. If your company hasn't defined a thorough sales process, this chapter is for you.

Important: Remember, you are a professional who helps people make purchasing decisions. As a professional, you need to learn how to help people effectively. Work to gain skills as an expert. Discover how businesses and people make purchases, which frequently changes over time.

Some experts believe that if potential customers have at least seven opportunities to turn down an offer during a sales pitch, but don't, the likelihood increases that those people will buy a product or service. I fully support that belief.

Here's why. If a potential customer isn't interested in a product or service, he or she can turn down your offer during your meeting. If they don't, they are implying their interest, because they want more information. If there are seven opportunities, one after another, and every time the potential customer conveys interest without turning down your offer, the possibility of the potential customer making a purchase heightens.

Having considered that concept, we should now discuss the ins and outs of the sales process. Here is an example of a sales process that one of my clients had before he and I began meeting.

The client's potential customers would request landscaping services. The client's salesperson would have a brief meeting with those people, and then the client would follow up and email a proposal. The entire sales process took two steps: having a meeting and sending a proposal. Following this method, the client won fewer than 10% of all proposals, and the ones he did get were low-margin, low-value projects for which he gave the lowest bid.

Within three months of creating a seven-plus sales step system, the client's conversion rate went from 1-in-10 to 1-in-4. It was a jump from a 10% conversion rate to a 25% conversion rate, and all it took was a change in the sales process. By the way, that increase was a difference of 150% in terms of the conversion rate. Therefore, the top-line revenue increased by 150% without the business investing much.

The client and I applied a variety of sales skills of higher value than the ones he was using, and ultimately, we moved the conversion rate to a number above 50% within months. All this success came when the client became a master of sales.

Creating a simple and good sales process is not complicated. Here is how I would start working with a client who didn't have one. First, I'd make sure the client understood the need for a process with seven or more steps. We know the last step will be the closing step, but I prefer to call this step "enrolling" or "onboarding" instead of "closing." The word "close" means to shut, separate, or stop. That description does not match what we want to see at this stage. Instead, we want to bring on a new client for ongoing sales activities.

Step 1:

This step will be the interview. The lead has come to the business, and it is an actual inquiry for your product or service. It is not a potential lead; it is a real lead. You have the person's contact information, which means a minimum of the name, the phone number, and the email address. Depending on your business, you might also have the title, the business name, the industry, and the necessary product or service solution. An example is a website design company that receives an email from someone asking about pricing for a website. If the company cultivates the lead accurately, the potential lead will convert to a real lead after the team asks these specific questions and perhaps a few more.

The interview is the first time the salesperson and the prospective client have a conversation. It could take place over the phone, in person, via email or even text message. This first step helps build rapport. It allows the salesperson to ascertain what the future client wants, and it lets both the salesperson and the prospective client determine if there is a potential fit. Note that the business must document this and every step with well-defined, useful scripts. During Step 1, the salesperson should outline the entire enrollment process and help the future customer decide what and how to purchase if he or she desires to do so.

Step 2:

This step of the sales process could be a short, yet thorough questionnaire that the prospective client completes. It could be simple or complex, but it should emulate the diagnosis stage at a doctor's office. In other words, it should be when the business learns what the client wants and determines what the client needs.

Wants and needs are essential concepts. A prospective client wants something to happen, whether that is to own a beautiful yard, to relieve back pain, to find a lovely centerpiece for an upcoming wedding, or to eat a tasty burger for lunch.

Underneath the want, there is a need. It is what the client must do or possess to get what he or she wants. A concept organizations worldwide follow is "understand what people want, and then sell them what they need."

The landscaping company might determine what the client wants through the questionnaire and an in-person meeting. These moments would help the business thoroughly understand the client's project, build rapport with the client, and establish credibility. At the same time, the company would need to make it clear that value rather than price should be the driving factor.

Step 3:

This step could be an email confirmation of the meeting that took place. It would contain a few links to a testimonial website and a reminder about the next appointment. At this point, it should be clear to the customer how the buying decision will happen, because the salesperson will have outlined the process for them to buy.

Step 4:

This step is the follow-up call or visit. It is the opportunity to see if the prospect is serious about your product or service. This follow-up experience can be a phone call, an email, or an in-person visit. When you create steps with a goal in mind, this step will be the pivot point. Either you will pivot and make changes to earn the prospect's business or the prospective customer will pivot and show more interest or less interest.

Step 5:

Now starts the final stretch of your sales process. At this point, you might be thinking this is a long and drawn-out process that isn't necessary. Indeed, if you are direct and quick to get to the point in most situations, this process might seem lengthy. However, if you are steady and cautious, this process might match what you would want as a customer. Remember, the buyer's personality and behavior are as important as the purchase-making language he or she speaks.

To complete Step 5, provide any exclusive deals or value offers that your business has on the product or service that the prospect wants. An example of a value offer is a deal, such as: buy X and get Y free. By the way, "free" is the best four-letter F-word on the planet. Everyone likes to get things for free, and if you can include something for free, it frequently will improve the purchasing decision.

A freebie does not have to be anything substantial. Think about a McDonald's Happy Meal™. It includes a small toy that costs the company nothing more than a few cents to make. For many children, the toy is the actual reason to make the purchase. The toy is only available in that particular meal. That means the meal includes items that some customers might not buy otherwise were it not for the toy.

Perhaps a landscaper could include a dozen periwinkle flowers with every $500 purchase. It would cost the company $10 for supplies and $5 for labor. Therefore, it would cost the company $15, but it would be a $100 value to the buyer. Offering this "free" deal would be an excellent way for the landscaping company to increase its value in the buyer's eyes.

No matter what value-added offer you propose, you still want to communicate to the buyer that you wish to complete his or her entire project. For example, the landscaper would create the "plan" — as opposed to the "proposal." (We are always assuming the sale will occur, thus the word "plan" over "proposal.")

Step 6:

In this step, you will confirm the meeting to review the proposal, preferably in person. At this stage, you and the customer might refine the proposal. By now, what the customer wants must be clear. There should be no doubt about it. You will have delivered your plan, which you used to call a proposal, and you will have provided the elements of the project, including the value proposition — the reason the client wants the work done.

Important: The "want" is the desirable outcome from the customer's perspective. The "need" is what the seller designates as the product or service that the business can deliver once the customer makes a purchase.

Step 7:

In this step, you can ask your prospective customer, "What would you like to do now?" You will have already provided all the appropriate information to help the person make a knowledgeable purchase. Still, the customer might have questions. If the prospective customer asks questions at this point, it means you are in the home stretch, because the person most likely wants to buy your product or service.

Hire Slowly, but Fire Quickly

Organizations are wise to remember that their team is the biggest reason for their success. The sales team is critical, because businesses cannot make money until they sell something. Keeping each Pillar of the business strong is an element of success, and it's imperative to look closely at the maintenance of the Sales Pillar. Let's do that now.

The business will measure the sales team on activity and results. Therefore, hire and train with these elements in mind. A great salesperson needs the energy to be a rainmaker, someone who secures deals or "closes," which as I mentioned previously, is an unfortunate term. The person needs the energy to make calls, meet for follow-ups, and reach daily goals. Does the person have energy that can increase with encouragement? If not, it will be hard for this person to do well in this job. When hiring salespeople, look for the energy they exude and the energy they seem to acquire as time passes. Some people exude energy, while others gather energy from other people. A good sales team will shine with positive energy. Hiring a team member who tends to be an energy gatherer means you might miss out on finding a rock-star salesperson. Pay attention to energy.

A great salesperson is someone who understands that the business needs results. For the right person, this element of the job will be exciting.

On the DISC scale, a person who ranks well in the D or I sections might be an ideal salesperson. The Ds aim for success every day. The Is of the world are friendly and outgoing, characteristics that help them build rapport and trust with prospective customers. A combination of these profiles showcases a candidate who could be successful as a salesperson, especially if that person receives proper training, has self-motivation, understands expectations, and the organization's definition of success. With every upside, there is a usual downside. In this case, the I/D person will likely be a low C, which means he or she won't be great at completing sales reports, documenting the

CRM, or doing paperwork for your operations. As you grow your team, consider having sales assistants help your rock-star salesperson reach new success levels. This sales assistant would be someone who ranks well in the C category.

It would be great to have several people who have I/D behaviors. Manage them well and hold them accountable, so that they can improve over time. Managing a team of this nature will be a challenge unless the team has a great manager, who most likely also has D/I or I/D traits.

Story: Years ago, my IT business expanded to Dallas, Texas, so I added a salesperson to my team. The new salesperson appeared to be a great hire.

He had many contacts and skills and seemed like an all-around impressive person. We gave him a company car, which was a nice SUV, and supported him with the tools to be successful in the technology sales space.

The new salesperson came to work every day and attended sales meetings, but after three months, he had no sales. The fourth month came and went, and he had some leads, but still no sales.

At six months, the situation was static, so a business consultant asked me when I would hold the team member accountable. I thought it was a great question, and I agreed that I needed to take action.

I asked another salesperson on the team how the new salesperson seemed to be doing, and I received positive feedback. Reportedly, the new salesperson did, after all, have several leads that had yet to convert, and he expected to get several new clients within weeks.

So, the dilemma continued. Would I keep the new salesperson for a few more weeks, or would I cut bait?

Well, I was still a little bit of a laissez-faire leader at that time, so I made the unfortunate decision not to change anything for two months. After nearly a year of payroll and no sales whatsoever, I decided to let the salesperson go.

Within two days, I discovered the person had been working another job that split his focus the entire time he worked for me! Wow, was I duped.

"Hire slowly, but fire quickly." This saying is a smart one. My hiring blunder was a $50,000 education experience. Hopefully, you'll learn from my mistakes and not repeat them.

Tip: As you bring on new salespeople, make sure they hit their target KPIs within the first 30, 60, and 90 days. Don't keep someone on the team if the person is like the new hire in the story above and cannot hit goals and targets. Never draw out the situation longer than 90 days. Then, if you part ways with a team member, fill the vacancy quickly.

Sales Pillar Continued

Conversion has many elements, some of which you will see here. Remember, prospective customers can find information about you and your business on the web; therefore, they will know about you long before you can make a deal. If you were to research everything online about your company, what would you see?

Start with social media platforms — Facebook, LinkedIn, Twitter, Instagram, and Yelp. What does your social media presence say about you and your company? Go to a computer that you haven't used to log in to these accounts and see what appears.

You might be surprised to see that each social media platform has something negative about you. New clients will and should vet what you say and what others say about you. For this reason, be sure every comment has a comment from the business or even you, the business owner. It doesn't matter what happened. It only matters what people say, even when those people are anonymous.

Can you and the sales team do similar research on the prospective customer? Search for them on social media platforms and any other applicable websites.

When it comes to speaking in another person's language, make sure there is plenty of progress.

Remember that four-quadrant behavior pattern opposites tend to have difficulty communicating with each other. Your job as a salesperson, sales manager, or business owner is to identify your clients' four-quadrant behavior pattern profile and accurately speak that language. It is not a challenging task to consider, but it isn't easy in real life. It takes practice to master this skill. Remember that the D or C future client will want to trust you first and like you second. On the other hand, the I or S prospective customer will want to like you first and trust you second. Both trusting and liking are required, so know which is most important to achieve based on the four-quadrant behavior pattern.

Although summarizing the Sales Pillar is not entirely possible, here are some of the biggest takeaways. Know your company and each salesperson's conversion rate. Maintain the minimum KPIs, expect no less than the expected KPIs, and incentivize for exceeding the expected KPIs. Prospective customers will research you, so make sure they find great information. Then, do your homework on potential clients. Figure out who on the team is the best salesperson, and if it is the business owner, make sure there is an apprentice so that one day the owner can focus on other aspects of the business. Know and implement all the necessary strategies to maximize the conversion rate (i.e., the guarantees). Understand the terms "like" and "trust" and the differences between them. Last, but not least, send a welcome gift or note to new clients to impress them and win them as repeat customers.

WHAT NOW? ACTION STEPS.

- ❏ What are the advantages you can see in identifying the communication and behavioral patterns in your prospects, clients, and team members?

- ❏ Write down your seven or more steps that you can or currently have in place to help people professionally buy from you? Consider the steps or terms you need to modify or add in this process like on boarding and enrolling to increase conversion rate.

- ❏ Analyze your "want" and "need" in your sales process. How does it need to be revised or updated to match your product and desired profit margin?

- ❏ How do you monitor and measure the energy of your sales team?

- ❏ As the business owner or general manager what activities can you put in place to reinforce the level of energy needed for your business to be successful?

- ❏ Describe the process you have or could create to implement the DISC communication and behavioral system into your business.

CHAPTER 5:

THE OPERATIONS PILLAR

If you are a painter, it is painting. If you are a lawyer, it is practicing law. If you own a bakery, it is baking. For a business coach, it is coaching. All of this is the Operations Pillar of a business. It is most likely your favorite part of having a business, and it is a common blindspot for growing a successful business.

Lawyers might enjoy law. They might work hard to be the best lawyer possible. However, those traits are not necessarily indicative of someone who is a successful business owner. I've taught lawyer clients that it is better to hire and train employees to become great lawyers — conceivably better lawyers than even the firm's owner — while the firm's owner becomes excellent at marketing, sales, operations, and finances. Plus, the firm's owner should learn to grow a successful team. For a law firm to flourish, the firm's owner needs to be a rainmaker, generate great partnerships with other businesses, and become great at marketing, sales, systems, and leadership. Doing so will allow the company to prosper at levels higher than what the firm's owner ever imagined possible. It is not that the firm's owner shouldn't be good at law. Instead, it is that the firm's owner should build an excellent law firm full of great lawyers.

In this chapter, I will assume that you are good at your professional trade, be it baking, landscaping, teaching, or something else. Rather than help you gain skills specific to your occupation, I will help you understand areas in which you can improve the Operations Pillar of your business regardless of your industry.

You're Good at What You Do, Let's See How Good

Picture the following business strategies:
- Services: Brains by the Hour
- Manufacturing
- Middleman

First is the business that sells brains by the hour. In this category, you might find accounting firms; law firms; consulting companies; technology companies; or training, coaching, and teaching companies. Any business that charges by the hour would be in this category. Even if you have a product business, such as a marketing company where you charge for creating a product, like a brochure, business card, or website, you are effectively still a brains-by-the-hour business. You charge for a product based on a desirable profit margin on an hour of labor. As I mentioned earlier, I had a business in this category, and some of the critical things I learned there I've shared throughout this book. I'll share new thoughts here.

Considerations for the "Services: Brains by the Hour" Business

Effectivity. Actual hours billed to clients divided by available hours equals a number called "effectivity." It is a spot where many brains-by-the-hour businesses miss out on profit and revenue. An example is a five-person law firm where each staff member could bill 30 hours a week. Here, you would see 150 billable hours per week as the denominator. If the law firm were to bill 50 hours in one week (i.e., the numerator), the effectivity rate would be 33% (i.e., 50 hours ÷ 150 billable hours). Knowing your effectivity rate is fundamental at a brains-by-the-hour company.

At my IT company, the effectivity rate reached 105%. It was marvelous! I'll explain how it happened later. First, consider the successes of a 50-person firm with 40% effectivity versus a 50-person firm with 105% effectivity. On the surface, there is a 65% increase in revenue. Examine the following table:

	50-person firm, 65% effectivity	50-person firm, 105% effectivity
Overhead (at $80k/year)	$4,000,000	$4,000,000
Bonus	$0	$200,000 (.05 x overhead)
Annual Revenue (at $85/hour)	$5,746,000	$9,282,000
Gross Profit Per Person	$34,920	$101,640

Change in Profit Per Person	66% decrease	191% increase
Gross Profit	$1,746,000	$5,082,000
Change in Gross Profit	Decrease of $3,336,000	Increase of $3,336,000

Another take might be to ask how this company generates revenues of $9,282,000 when the team has 65% effectivity. Here are the numbers with higher costs to team members:

	81-person firm 65% effectivity
Overhead (at $80k/year)	$6,480,000
Bonus	$0
Annual Revenue (at $85/hour)	$9,308,520
Gross Profit Per Person	$34,920
Gross Profit	$2,828,520
Change in Gross Profit from a company with 105% effectivity	44% decrease equals $2,253,480 less profits with significantly more overhead**

*Eighty-one people at $85 per hour at 2,080 hours per year at 65% effectivity equals $9.3 million.

** This illustration does not count the extra management and overhead required to add 31 more people (i.e., 62% additional staff).

Many people have an inadequate understanding of effectivity, and therefore manage it poorly. It is one of many areas where I learned how to give significant bonuses to team members, and it allowed me to be more successful in my business. So, how did I get to 105%? Here is what I did. Maybe you can do it as well.

We had a great product and a great attitude, and clients loved us. As a result, clients wanted more of our product, so we gained billable hours.

The option was to hire more people or give hours to the team. Typically, a consulting company pays a fixed salary to team members, and any billable hours go to the company.

There are training costs and overhead expenses, all of which suck up profits. But employees billing a 40-hour workweek covered our profit margins. (Actually, just 36 hours covered our overhead and profit.)

So, when the opportunity arose to hire, train, and manage additional people, I instead asked the existing team, "Do you want more hours? If so, I'll give you bonuses for any billed hours over 40 hours."

The team was ecstatic! What first seemed like a problem became a boom to our business. We were not short-staffed after all. Our staff became busier, our effectivity rate soared above 120% month over month, and our profits flew through the roof. Plus, our actual overhead remained consistent, allowing a decrease in overhead per billable hour and an increase in Gross Profit margin.

Now, if these numbers make you dizzy, don't worry. I will address this topic again in the Finance Pillar.

Cash Gap. Knowing the number of days that you have a negative cash flow during any measurable time is a typical blindspot for businesses in the service industry. It is common to pay for labor costs, overhead, and other expenses long before you collect from the client. Sometimes you pay again and again for things before a client pays you. I experienced that situation in one of my previous businesses, and it was a tremendous problem even when profits were soaring. Let me explain.

Personal Story. When I began my technology business, the most I could earn in a year was $250,000. When I was billing $125 per hour, and when I billed 40 hours per week, it worked out to roughly $250,000 of personal income in one calendar year. Eventually, I hired and trained an effective team that always kept busy. Profits were terrific. At the peak of my technology business, we were earning $250,000 in profit each month. The P&L statement looked remarkable. I was able to make 12 times my maximum, because I went from being a solo entrepreneur (also known as a fantastic programmer) to a good business owner.

We were busy every day. Our in-house accountant, our human resources and training team, our project management team, and everyone else always had work. The team rocked and I will always be grateful to those people.

Being busy all the time came with unique challenges. The cash gap, which I did not fully understand yet, was a negative game-changer. Payroll was $250,000 twice a month. The large clients who paid slowly seemed to be the only clients we had. Plus, we did not yet invoice properly, as I had yet to learn how to do so. Little did I know, disaster loomed around the corner, and I needed to make changes.

At one point, I knew I had reached dire straits when I was supposed to pay $250,000 of payroll, but had only $50,000 in the bank. I needed $200,000, but the bank wouldn't loan me more money. I had a house worth almost $1 million, but I had mortgaged it twice; so, I couldn't do anything there. I had maxed out a personal line of credit worth $1 million, so I had no wiggle room there either. I had an accounts receivable list worth nearly $3 million, but, as I mentioned, all our clients seemed to pay slowly. My product, which was my team, needed to pay bills. Plus, they were working tirelessly to satisfy clients, which were Fortune 50 companies we had to keep happy. We had discovered our biggest business blindspot, a huge cash gap.

After moments of frustration and panic, we found a solution from a business-consulting company that had seen this type of situation before. Upon our request, the company swooped in and saved the day. An expert from the company charged us $35,000 to create a spreadsheet within an entire system to solve our cash gap problem. The spreadsheet compared the number of days that we paid money to the number of days that we received money.

When your payroll is $500,000 per month, and your cash gap is 125 days, you will be $1,500,000 short, because you didn't receive payment from the clients. In this case, we sent out invoices totaling $2,225,000, showing a $750,000 profit over the 125 days. However, regardless of the profits, you'll need $1,500,000 in the bank or available lines of credit to finance the business, even when the profit numbers are high. It happens, because cash leaves the company faster than it appears. When a company scales up quickly, that situation can happen, and it had occurred to my company. Here is what I learned about this business blindspot.

1. Send invoices quickly, and make sure clients receive them. At our company, we had become careless about organizing timesheets and lazy about sending invoices to clients. We were in denial that half of the clients regularly said they could not find an invoice two months after we were supposed to have received a payment. It turned out these aspects of the problem took up 29 of our 125-day cash gap. Those issues were in our control, so we implemented changes. We demanded that team members complete timesheets by 10 p.m. each Friday of each week.

Failure to complete the task was not an option. If a team member failed to submit a timesheet, he or she would not receive payment on time, as we had to submit payroll by the time we had designated. All invoicing processes, including the proofreading by and approval from managers, finished on Tuesdays. We then sent invoices the next day and confirmed their receipt within three business days. These solutions helped us invoice clients quickly and secure payments sooner than later.

2. When confirming that a client received an invoice, our accountant asked the client to share the date on which we would receive payment. This question became part of the accountant's script. It was just another standard question, so it felt comfortable to ask. Once we had the information, we entered it on a 13-week cash flow forecast spreadsheet, which the business-consulting expert built. We updated that document each week, and in doing so, we knew when money would arrive and when it would leave. By asking the client or the client's accounts payable (AP) department questions, we gathered a lot of information. For example, we learned who had to approve invoices at each company. We also learned when approval processes took place, as well as when check runs occurred, which dramatically changed when we received payments. The term "check run" is an accounting department expression that means the time when the business will print checks that are due. Frequently, companies have check runs once or twice a month. It was helpful information for us to have.

We even learned how each client's system paid vendors based on "terms" that the AP department entered, which by the way, never seemed to match the terms in our agreements.

3. Our clients raved about us. They were our fans and we had a fantastic team that provided the results that our clients wanted. Therefore, we felt comfortable enough to ask for better terms. Yes, these were enormous companies, but enormous companies are, after all, groups of people who deserve great treatment. We treated people with respect, so they updated their computer systems to send us payments more quickly. Have you ever sent donuts to the AP department of your largest client? We did. It made the AP department's day, and they then moved payments along faster than ever. You must remember who at a company controls the purse strings.

4. We had improved our internal invoicing processes and our relationships with our clients' AP departments. So, when it was possible, we began invoicing clients weekly with 10-day terms. Not everyone accepted the new terms, but those who did helped us reduce our cash gap to 30 days. Therefore, the cash gap dropped by three days on average. Think three days isn't much? Here is the math: 120 days is $3,000,000. Divide 120 days by three days and get 40 days. Now, divide $3,000,000 by 40 days. You get $75,000. That means we had an extra $75,000 in the bank

all the time, because we reduced the cash gap by three days.

5. Next, we changed our payroll. Before the change, we paid biweekly on Fridays, which added up to 26 payments per year. We also paid staff members for hours they worked through the Monday of payroll week. We then changed payday to the 15th day of the month and the last day of the month, reducing the number of payments per year to 24. We paid wages for timesheets from the end of the previous period, and we held one payroll check. This practice is a standard payroll procedure for many companies, but it was new to us. Eventually, the change meant a reduction of 10 days of the cash gap. Here is more math. We regained $25,000 for each day that the cash gap decreased, so in this case, we picked up $250,000.

6. If possible, use a paperless invoicing processing system for your largest client so that you can use electronic invoicing and automated clearing house (ACH) payments. We called our paperless invoicing processing system "PIPS" for short. When working with us, our largest client needed to use our PIPS, because it received too many late fees from other companies. It had faced issues with the bank pausing business credit cards when executives tried to use them during business trips abroad, which effectively left the executives stranded without money. For this reason, the client asked to use our PIPS to allow for fast internal approval and quick ACH bank-to-bank payments. We had

developed the system, so we became the test subjects to show how rapidly payments could happen with our PIPS. When we submitted an invoice before noon, it received approval and payment processed the same day. Therefore, we had just a day of turnaround time from invoicing to cash in the bank, and we loved it.

7. Get deposits for all projects. When you list payment terms in your contracts with clients, cover this point. Your client might want to negotiate with you. Rest assured that taking a deposit is a common practice in many industries, and your client might take deposits for products and services, too.

There are many other ways to improve the cash gap. Dell Computers has a great example. Dell collects payments from buyers before it begins to make the product and then pays vendors in 30 to 45 days. Therefore, Dell has a negative cash gap and makes money on the customer's money while producing the product.

Speaking of deposits, here is another example of getting paid early. When Tesla announced its Model 3 electric car for sale, it included delivery to occur in 18 to 36 months. Customers had to submit a down-payment deposit of $1,000. Then, customers received a reservation number based on their placement in the queue with other buyers. In that order, Tesla produced the cars with the unique specifications each customer wanted. The product launch turned out to be one of the biggest retail sales days ever. The company received more than 300,000 orders. Immediately, Tesla had $300,000,000 of unearned revenue from deposit money. Plus, the average Model 3 cost the consumer around $45,000, so Tesla's recorded sales that day were in the area of $18 billion.

Considerations for the "Manufacturing" Business.

A manufacturing business is any business that produces a product and then sells it. It is the typical "widget" business. The term "widget" can mean any product — a pen, a pad of paper, an office chair, a desk, a TV, a couch, a computer, a keyboard, a guitar, shingles for a roof, grass for a lawn, seeds at a plant nursery, donuts at a bakery, or any other tangible product. These are all widgets that are part of an inventory. The business that makes those goods is a manufacturing business.

Knowing your profit margins on each product you sell seems like a common-sense strategy. However, I have coached many manufacturing clients, and not one has known its profit margins on each product sold before I've asked for that information. Yes, some knew other margins, but none has ever known which of its products had the most significant margin or dollar of profit per product sold.

For example, a bakery I coached knew it made a 65% profit margin on every donut it sold. However, the company didn't know how much profit margin was in every coffee that people bought. It also didn't know which of its products earned the highest profit for the business each time someone bought it. A $1 donut had a $.65 of profit, or 65% profit margin. What was better than that was the $3.75 smoothie the company sold. It earned the donut shop $2 of profit, which turned out to be a 53% profit margin.

With that new knowledge, the company now makes better decisions with its marketing and upselling efforts. Rather than asking, "Would you like a milk or coffee with your donut," a clerk might ask, "Have you tried one of our amazing and refreshing smoothies, and if not, could I offer you a free sample?" The customer would probably love the smoothie and buy one. In this sale, the profit would increase by $2. In comparison, selling a coffee would have raised the profit per sale by $1 or less per sale. Therefore, the profits per sale could double.

Again, effectivity is an excellent measurement opportunity for the manufacturer. Imagine a small bakery that has an oven. How effective is the oven? Let's say the oven operates 23 out of 24 hours to maximize its production. That leaves an hour a day for cleaning and maintenance. Losing 365 hours a year is equal to 4% downtime, which means uptime is 96%.

Many companies would look down on only having an uptime of 96%. Consider a computer or car being out of commission for 2.5 minutes of every hour. It would be unacceptable. However, it is unheard of for ovens to operate 23 out of the 24 hours in a day, especially at small bakeries. Therefore, this number is phenomenal, and the oven is extremely effective.

If we agree that the bakery could operate this special oven 23 out of the 24 hours in a day, 23 becomes the denominator of your utilization factor. All manufacturing companies have machines and tools that they use each day, and each one has a maximum usage limit per day.

Calculate the effectiveness of each machine or tool at your business. Working every quarter to increase the efficiency of your production will increase the overall profits of your company. Yes, there is a point of diminishing returns. The point at which you overuse something (or someone), you will get less favorable results. Therefore, businesses need to know these numbers.

Equipment utilization is a simple percentage of available hours or minutes. In the baker's oven example, 23 hours divided by 24 hours is 95.8%. It means that the equipment could operate 95.8% of the time. However, if you measure how much the oven is in use, you might see that the actual number is 10 hours a day. Therefore, the business would be underutilizing the oven by a significant amount.

Here is the math:

10 hours used divided by 23 hours available is 43.5%.

A smart business owner would work hard to increase the utilization of this oven before buying another oven. Nevertheless, a more common situation is that business owners purchase a new oven long before considering the utilization factor.

Now, let's consider the utilization of a team member. Use the same math, but smaller numbers. An accounting firm hires accounting staff to work 40 hours a week; however, the staff bills clients 20 hours per week on average. Thus, the utilization is 50%. Again, commonly, business owners in this situation will hire more team members before helping to increase the utilization rate of the team already in place.

In one of the businesses I built, we had an average utilization rate of 105%. That meant team members worked about 5% over their expected hours for our clients. We gave our employees bonuses for achieving our goal utilization rate, which worked out well. By working on utilization instead of hiring, we were able to save the manager time and give bonuses to our hard-working team.

The calendar is a huge cost for every manufacturer. In a coaching session, I had a client work out the calendar cost for his products. It was incredible — even shocking — how much it cost the client to house inventory.

Profits dropped 10% for each product that the client kept in inventory for an extra month. When you are earning about 30% on each product sold, keeping products in inventory for 30 days cuts profit margins 3%, as 10% of the 30% is 3%.

This client's experience is relevant to many business owners. In fact, many businesses keep products in inventory for an average of 45 to 90 days.

For this client, the 3% profit margin loss came off the bottom line. Every 30 days that the client's product remained unsold and in inventory, the bottom line dropped 3%.

Seeing these figures was a huge realization for the client. On average, the bottom line was 18%. Therefore, increasing the inventory turns from 60 days on average to 30 days on average raised the bottom line by 3%, a 16.7% increase in profits.

Let's see the math. Increasing profits by 3% and moving from 18% to 21% equals a 3% increase on the original 18%. Divide 3 by 18 and get a 16.66% improvement. Business owners pay attention when they see the opportunity to increase the company's bottom line by nearly 17%.

Fast inventory turn is critical whether the product is something the company produces or a raw good that a business uses for production. Work hard to know the calendar cost for each month that you have insurance, payroll, rent, dues, and fees, as well as interest and other monthly expenses. Don't let the calendar eat up your profits.

Considerations for a "Middleman" Business

Businesses that buy products and resell them fit in this category. It is the category with clothing shops, grocery stores, gas stations, and convenience stores. Direct sales companies — both multi-level marketing and MLMs — fall into this category. It encompasses all companies that purchase products at wholesale prices and sell them at new retail prices. It's the companies that buy low and sell high.

Here is an example of an inventory turn that illustrates one strategy for this category. A client of mine sold a popular energy drink. He usually bought 1,000 cans at a time and paid $2 per can. Then, he sold each can for $3 and made $1 in profit. One day, he purchased a large stock of 5,000 cans, because the product was on sale. However, he continued selling at a rate of no more than four cans per day, or about 120 cans per month.

Nevertheless, the client made the purchase — without discussing it with his business coach first — and acquired enough product to last him 41 months, which is longer than three years. Initially, he doubled his profit on this product and went from making about $120 per month to making about $240 per month. He invested $5,000 to make the extra $120 per month. Together, he and I calculated the break-even time. The $5,000 investment divide by the $240 profit per month equaled 20.8 months, or just short of two years.

Unfortunately, this client was a compulsive shopper who leapt at wholesale discounts to make more money per retail sale. The client put all the cash toward inventory and went broke.

If the client had learned the power of inventory turn, he might have made more than $2 per sale over 21 months.

Here is the math:

Invest $240 per month to purchase 120 cans. Sell them for $360, and profit $120. Repeat this strategy for 21 months, and get $2,520 on an investment of $240, which repeats monthly.

Furthermore, profits from the first two months fund the entire 21 months. So, invest $240 for two months (i.e., $480) and get $2,040 — a 425% return on investment.

The other option has an initial investment of $5,000. You can't pay it back for 13.8 months. At 21 months, profits are $10,000 — a 200% return on investment.

Of course, a 425% return is much better than a 200% return. Plus, it translates into money that the business can direct toward other smart inventory purchases.

Knowing All Your Numbers. Every business can benefit from knowing the numbers. Consider the number of leads and the conversion rate. Think about the average dollar per sale. Find the busiest hour of the day and the busiest day of the week, and then look from the opposite angle, and find the slowest hour and the slowest day. Which marketing efforts do and don't work? Those are part of the numbers. There are many numbers every business must consider, and business owners who avoid the responsibility of reviewing numbers set the company up for mediocrity. Conversely, success comes when a business owner embraces numbers, learns what they mean, and lets them inform decisions that support aspirations and goals. One of our clients worked with us for three years.

Knowing your best salesperson. Who is the best cashier at your business? Who does the best at upselling and cross-selling, and who makes deals happen? Businesses, especially small ones, usually have one or two team members who stand out. Why are they at the top of the list? Company leaders must learn what makes some team members exceptional salespeople and then train everyone else to be as capable as their counterparts.

In the donut shop example that I mentioned, the best cashier was always the owner. The owner did the absolute best at upselling, cross-selling, and making the customer feel appreciated. In that case, the owner needed to invest time with the order-taking team's leaders and help them improve. When this happened, great results occurred. When the owner didn't put in extra effort to train the team, sales suffered. Get the best cashier to teach the other team members. Incentivize this rock-star team member to help the rest of the team improve.

How and why do customers buy repeatedly? One important factor is "delivery mastery." I learned about delivery mastery from ActionCOACH™. It is the foundation of the "6-Steps to Build a Great Business," an ActionCOACH™ model that Brad Sugars and his team created. Having used this model for the last decade, I find that the one thing that keeps coming to mind is that I wish I had learned about it sooner than I did.

Delivery mastery is providing a consistent product and delivering it to the customer in a consistent manner every time. You, too, can create consistency in delivering your product and service. There are four primary areas of delivery mastery: supply mastery, quality mastery, ease-to-buy mastery, and service mastery.

Rank your business on how well it meets the following statements on a scale from 1 to 10, with 10 being the best.

- We continuously work to improve our product delivery.
- We use surveys to ask our customers how we are doing.
- We evaluate the responses and address them to improve customer satisfaction.
- We monitor team members on customer satisfaction.
- We document procedures and use a flowchart to guide decisions.
- We have scripts to help us greet customers.
- The team brainstorms ways to exceed customer expectations.

By consistently working on delivery mastery, you will grow a client base by creating raving fans. Be sure to read *Raving Fans* by Ken Blanchard and Sheldon Bowles. This book will help you and your team understand why raving fans are essential for every successful business.

Supply Mastery. Some years ago, at my technical services company, one of my staff members noticed that a competitor of ours undercut us on the price of a product. The competitor quoted half the price of what we quoted for the same thing. We knew from our research that the competitor didn't even have the product in stock. It worked out in our favor, because customers saw through the competitor's false advertisements. The competitor couldn't supply the product, and we were right there to pick up the business.

We provided a great product at a value-based price, so the customer stayed with us, and the competition disappeared.

Here are some questions and thoughts on supply mastery:

1. Can customers get what they buy?
2. Is delivery on time?
3. Can the company consistently make, buy, or deliver the products and services?
4. Basic delivery is vital for growth.
5. How much of a sales increase can you handle?
6. You don't want to lose customers through bad delivery.
7. Consistency of delivery is the goal.

Quality Mastery

We've all seen products and services of inferior quality. Maybe it's a defective used car, a meal that gives a person food poisoning, or luggage that gets lost in the airport. The problem might not exist if someone had paid better attention. A small change could prevent a non-returning customer from becoming a vocal, unhappy heckler to your business.

Questions and thoughts on quality mastery:

1. There is no way to get customers back if you can't deliver what they buy at the standard they expect.
2. Delivering what you promise helps you grow.
3. Are you losing customers due to low quality?
4. What areas do you deliver well, and where do you struggle?
5. Investigate customer complaints.
6. Mystery shop.
7. Make sure the customer gets what they bought.

Ease-to-Buy Mastery

At one of my former businesses, we purchased a lot of IT hardware on business credit cards from American Express. A local, reasonably large supplier of products we used did not take American Express. We loved Amex, because it helped us produce expense reports and track purchases, tasks that were difficult and time-consuming if I used personal credit cards. So, in the end, we stopped shopping at the place that didn't take Amex, and we spent more than $1,000,000 on hardware and software at other retailers.

CHAPTER 5: THE OPERATIONS PILLAR

Questions and thoughts to consider on ease-to-buy mastery:

1. Many companies make it too hard to buy.
2. The customer never wants to hear you say, "But it's our policy."
3. Keep things easy to understand.
4. Make sure things are easy to find.
5. Display things in a way that is easy to see.
6. Ensure an easy payment process.
7. Make returning easy and rewarding.
8. Hire mystery shoppers.
9. Use customer surveys.
10. Have common sense.

Service Mastery

The last area of mastery is service mastery. Who do you know who provides great service? At the top of my list are probably Southwest Airlines, Nordstrom, and Zappos. Southwest Airlines sings "Happy Birthday" to people on their birthday. It is a little bit embarrassing, but it is fun. Nordstrom has an incredible return policy. The company prefers a receipt, but does not make a big deal about it. I once returned a pair of shoes to Nordstrom after a year, because the black leather had turned gray. I didn't have the receipt, but Nordstrom honored my return and let me replace the shoes with a brand new pair, all without my original receipt. Zappos built its entire business model on helping the customer no matter what. It will help you find the product you want, even if you need to go to a competitor. Each of these examples shows customer service that leads to raving fans and long-term business.

Is your company receiving rave reviews, praise, and recommendations from clients? You want and need raving fans in order to be a successful company. If you are not receiving frequent comments from happy clients, you need to rethink your position.

So, we ask, "What does the raving fan's experience look like?" Don't hold back with your ideas. Capture the description of the experience, and then make it happen day after day.

Questions and thoughts to consider on service mastery:

1. How do you measure your level of customer service?
2. Be sure the basics of a smile and good service are in place.
3. Where are you losing business because of bad service?
4. Does the solution need a fresh set of eyes?
5. Train people to care.
6. Replace people who don't care about service.
7. Common sense will prevail.

Consistently working on your delivery mastery will grow your client base, because you will create raving fans. By turning customers into raving fans, you create repeat customers who direct a lot of revenue and other customers your way and revolutionize your business.

Your Best Customers are Raving Fans

If an airline were to upgrade you on a flight, you would probably tell your friends and family. In doing so, you would become a raving fan. Sometimes, airlines do upgrade people. It is one of the airline's efforts to make you a raving fan. Too often the opposite is true. People rant and rave about bad products or services, and they want the world to know. People occasionally tell a couple of friends or family members about a wonderful experience. On the other hand, people will post on the internet, call everyone they know, and do their best to threaten the reputation of a business that caused a problem.

We want happy clients who tell the world good things about us. When customers are unhappy, we want them to tell us and us alone. Then we can fix the problem quickly and avoid any damage to our reputation.

How do you create raving fans? It starts with simple things like under-promise and over-deliver. Never over-promise and under-deliver. I remember my dad telling me when I was delivering pizzas at 16 years old, always tell people you'll be there five to 10 minutes later than you expect. When you arrive early, customers will be surprised and pleased. If you arrive later than you expect yet you are still on time according to what you promised customers, they will still happy. It is a simple concept most businesses overlook.

I recently booked a flight overseas for business and I decided to use airline miles to upgrade from coach to business class. To do so, I had to purchase a seat in coach and wait to see if any business-class seats remained available at the time of the flight so that I could upgrade. I booked my trip 90 days in advance, and at that time, 46 of the 48 business-class seats were available. Each week leading up to the trip, I checked how many other people had booked seats in business class. Slowly but surely, all business class seats filled. I knew I would have to spend the 17-hour flight in coach.

However, a client suggested that I write to the CEO of the airline, so I did. I sent an email to the CEO of this large airline company. Surprisingly, I received a reply from the executive staff within a day, and after some back and forth, we scheduled a phone call and talked three days later. I explained my situation, which the executive staff couldn't solve, as other people already had bought all the business class seats.

Nevertheless, the executive staff listened to me and agreed that it would be wise to make upgrades possible when business-class seats first became available. They promised to work on it. I didn't get what I wanted, but it still seemed like I had made a difference, and the company would solve the problem. A couple of months later, I had to take another business trip to the same place overseas, so I booked the same flight on the same carrier, and I had feared the same situation would happen.

However, when I entered the online booking portal to book my flight, I found that I could use my miles to upgrade to business class instantly. Of the 48 seats in business class, 43 were available when I booked my ticket, but I didn't have to wait to upgrade and the system allowed me to take care of it immediately. Sending an email to the CEO had worked. The executive staff had listened to my opinion and made the change that we had discussed. They had made me a raving fan.

There are dozens of ways to turn everyday customers into raving fans. It takes just an hour or so each month to think of new ways to delight customers and create positive experiences that they will talk about with other people. Brainstorm with your team. Ask your customers what they want. Commit to solving issues. These steps will help you create happy customers and turn them into raving fans.

DOUG WINNIE

Measure what percent of your customers are raving fans. How many clients gave you a five-star review in the past month, quarter, or year? Divide that number by your total number of paying customers, and you get your raving-fan ratio (RFR). If you have 500 customers and seven provided a five-star review, you divide seven by 500 and get a 1.4% RFR. You would need to work to increase that figure to 2% by the next quarter and 3% by the next quarter. Ultimately, you would get your RFR to 5%. You would see new customers, because 1 in 20 customers would be a raving fan who did the selling for you.

Operations Systemized and Optimized

You've become good at what you do. That's great! Now, duplicate yourself with team members. Ensure everyone who interacts with your business has a stellar experience, even when you're not there. You can get to this point with excellent operations that you document and systemize well.

Let's use the law firm example again.

What is the system a law firm uses to gather the information from a prospective client? Do the staff members use the same script every time? Do they have a process to follow? Would the firm's owner ask questions with the same tone, pitch, and volume as a new associate who underwent training a month ago? Based on my experience coaching several lawyers and law firms, the answer is a big no.

Let's say this law firm specializes in family law. In this example, the firm's owner is a lawyer who is almost magical in her ability to talk to a prospective client about a case. She asks all the right questions and comments in just the right way. She helps prospective customers see that there isn't a better family law attorney on the planet.

Now, let's say a prospective client hears about the law firm from a friend. The prospective client decides to hire the firm's owner before the soon-to-be-ex does. So, the prospective client calls the firm and asks to speak with the firm's owner.

Unfortunately, the firm's owner is in court with a different client, so she can't take calls. Instead, the new client reaches an associate who has been with the firm for three months. The new associate now must help the prospective client until the firm's owner returns.

With excellent training and thorough scripts and processes, the new associate will do just as well as the firm owner would do in this situation. The associate will impress the prospective client who will decide to work with the firm even without the firm's owner, the rainmaker, having to be present.

Businesses can benefit from the use of scripts. Make scripts. Instruct staff members on how to use them. Then, have role-playing exercises to help the staff members practice the scripts.

You can systemize specific ways to handle different situations. In business, although each situation is unique, the 80/20 Pareto Principle is applicable; systemize 80% using scripts and checklists, and leave 20% for the team to provide a unique experience to the situation.

If you own a dental practice, document how you want the other dentists to perform the tasks you've mastered. Then train those other dentists.

Remember, in super successful businesses, the business owner does not do most of the work. Instead, the business owner no longer works in the business every day, because team members do most of the work. In this situation, checks keep coming in for the business owner, who is no longer near the business on a day-to-day basis or at all.

A great test is if the owner doesn't come in one day. If you, the business owner, didn't go to work tomorrow, what would happen? Would the team close down for the day? Would the team go with the flow, because they had enough training? Would the team panic about your absence or would they think it not a big deal? Hopefully, the day would progress like any other day, and the team would not have any major issues.

The following are a few more examples to systemize your business. If your business category isn't listed, create a list of your own with several of these strategies:

- A home remodeler has a measurement system to measure all the walls, floors, and ceilings of a home.
- A plumber follows a 13-point check system, which includes upselling a special service for the plumbing in kitchens.
- A landscaper uses a tablet program to record all dying plants in clients' gardens, and this process helps the sales team follow up with deals.
- A marketing company uses a seven-point checklist to determine the possible ROI for a prospective client's marketing investments.
- A delivery company uses three GPS systems to identify the best routes and rewards delivery drivers who use the least amount of gas.

WHAT NOW? ACTION STEPS.

- ❑ Have you identified your cash gap in your business? In which areas of the operations pillar does your business need to become more diligent and consistent?

- ❑ Which operations department (payable or receivable) needs to be restructured to achieve optimal results for their department?

- ❑ What is the profit margin on each product or service your business provides?

- ❑ What elements of your business need examining to improve the effectivity rate? How can you make plans to increase the effectivity rate for these elements?

- ❑ What areas in your business need more tracking of numbers? What methods can you put in place to achieve higher results?

- ❑ Of the four primary areas of delivery mastery (supply, quality, ease to buy, or service) which ones do you need to refine in order to improve operations and financial returns?

- ❑ Name the three to five strategies you currently have in place or could implement to maintain and build your "raving fan" relationships. What methods will you create and document to measure the effectiveness?

CHAPTER 6:

THE FINANCE PILLAR

This section is, perhaps, the most important, but it may be the weakest section for many business owners. We will look at three essential reports: P&L, cash flow, and Balance Sheet. I will also discuss Gross Profit margin per item sold, whether that item is a widget or an hour of labor. This chapter will explore ways to calculate break-even point by month, day, or even minute. You will leave this chapter and ask who is doing your books? You will see that you need to take the time to review your financials and make decisions about them monthly. Plus, you will get to know your industry's KPIs for productivity and effectivity. You will evaluate your company's goals, and you will consider the percent of every dollar that goes to materials, labor, overhead, and profit.

In my experience as a business owner and a business coach, finance is the Pillar that businesses understand and manage the worst. At the same time, it is the most important Pillar. It is a mistake to devote attention to operations, sales, teams, and marketing if a business fails to manage its finances. If a business loses money on every sale, should you just increase sales? No, you need to address the reason each sale loses money. If the cost of gaining a lead is more than the lifetime value of the customer, should you just get more leads? No, you need to rebalance that equation. If the business model isn't sound and there isn't a clear profit motive, fix those problems before working on other areas. Fix the financial foundation first.

A former client of mine, one of the first businesses I ever coached, ran on meager profit margins. Reviewing the financials, I saw that the company didn't get enough of a profit from each sale to cover the fixed cost of operations.

Marketing and sales numbers looked good. They found and added great staff members at a speedy pace, and everything else looked great, but they continued to lose money.

The situation worried me, the business coach, but it also upset the business owner's spouse, who funded the company and covered its losses. The business owner was excited about the increased business opportunities and future growth of the company. Bear in mind that this business did not have the potential to become the next Amazon.com. Instead, it was a standard brains-by-the-hour business, and it required more employees as it acquired customers.

I tried and failed to get the owner to raise prices or cut costs. Nothing worked. He seemed convinced that improving sales and improving operations would improve finances.

Ultimately, the business failed to improve its margins and neglected to change its business model. The business owner surrendered to the fact that the financials did not look good and never would. In this case, the maximum utilization for the business did not make the business successful. Years later, that business still operates at a loss, and the spouse still provides financial support for the company.

Important: Your business might be losing money when you have revenues of $300,000 or even $1,000,000 or more. It is critical to understand what is happening with the finances before you try to add revenue. I've seen attempts to add revenue increase losses many times, and I've also seen decreasing revenue make a company profitable. It is all in the finances. Understand break-even. Understand gross profit. Understand exactly how you make money on every sale.

Next, I'll describe some important terms and some caveats about each one.

Financials

Businesses utilize financial reports to determine if the organization is doing excellently, adequately, or poorly. These reports include the Income Statement, which many people call the Profit and Loss Statement (P&L), Balance Sheet, and Cash Flow Report.

Consider being a passenger on a flight. Instruments within the airplane help you get to your destination safely and on time. In business, the financials are the instruments that help you do business well.

The Cash Flow Report shows the fuel. The Income Statement reveals the level of safety at which the company operates. The Balance Sheet shows the health of the business.

If you ignore a report, you might face serious consequences. Conversely, fixating on one report will cause problems, too. Review the financials every month, whether you want to do it or not. Just like airplane pilots use the instruments available to them to improve a flight, a business owner should use instruments — reports in this case — to improve the business.

Break-even. The break-even point is where revenue equals all expenses. It also should include the amount of profit that the business owner desires. If break-even is $20,000 per month in revenue, and the desired profit for the year is $120,000, we would say the break-even is more than $30,000 per month. (I will define the term "more than" shortly.) When calculating break-even, include the profit that the business wants in the figure.

Accrual Accounting. Some places in the world use the metric system, while others use the imperial system. Both are accurate systems of measurement. They are just different. Similarly, there are two ways to run business reports: accrual accounting and cash-based accounting. The approaches are both valid, but different. Accrual accounting is when the business puts all appropriate data in the same period for reporting. For example, if you have sales in May, you must report May sales expenses in that same period. If you receive sales commissions a month later and report those sums in June, you inaccurately recorded the costs associated with the sale from May. Inaccuracies and bad data in this report can keep the business owner from making prudent decisions.

Cash-Based Accounting. The other accounting method, cash-based accounting, reports the cash that changes hands on a specific date. If you buy something on December 5, you record and report in December. If you send an invoice to a client in December and receive payment in January, record the revenue in January, not December, even though you completed the work in December. Most businesses with which we work operate on a cash basis for tax reporting. Most accounting and Certified Public Accountant (CPA) firms focus on tax reporting, so their biggest concerns are usually cash-based reports. Although many businesses tend to pay taxes on a cash basis, we run our company on the accrual accounting method. For us, accrual is the only real way to obtain accurate data to make sound business decisions.

Fixed Costs

Fixed costs are business expenses that stay the same each month. These expenses are things like rent, insurance, and payroll, which usually do not change. Fixed costs should increase as the business grows. For example, a business should add team members over time to decrease the business owner's tasks. If your fixed costs are not increasing, you are likely not growing.

Variable Costs

The amount necessary to make a sale entirely because of the sale itself is called the Variable Cost. It also is called the Cost of Goods Sold (COGS). In addition to being the material to produce a product or service, a Variable Cost might be a commission that a business pays salespeople who sell a product. It might be a transportation cost to deliver a product or service, or it might be a cost of labor to do a task. You'll note that Variable Costs should not change much as a percent of sales. However, they could decrease as you learn to make smart, strategic business purchases. Ideally, if you see Variable Costs around 30% this month, you should see a number around 30% next month. Proper accounting will demonstrate this point. Here is an example of how Variable Costs can get messy in your financials.

If you buy lumber for a furniture business, use it over the next three months and allocate the data over that time. So, if you buy the lumber in June and record all the costs in June, you should see steep Variable Costs in June and low Variable Costs in July and August. The correct way to track Variable Costs is to ask your accountant to use inventory, deposits, and accrual. I have outlined these terms here, and your accounting team will understand them. Alternatively, learn to track Variable Costs on your own by taking a course in accounting, reading books on the subject, or watching online video tutorials.

Gross Profit Margin

When you see the word "margin" in a term, it means the result will be a percent. Gross Profit is the dollar amount remaining from revenue when you subtract Variable Costs. Gross Profit margin is the percent of the profit remaining when you omit Variable Costs. For example, if you have revenue of $50,000 and Variable Costs of $20,000, the Gross Profit is $30,000 (i.e., $50,000 minus $20,000). Therefore, the Gross Profit margin is 60% (i.e., $50,000 minus $20,000, which is $30,000 divided by the $50,000 revenue).

I teach clients that it is not important to be a great accountant, but it is important to know how to read and understand financials and then use the data to make smart business decisions.

Income Statement. Recall that the Income Statement also goes by the name Profit and Loss Statement (P&L). It shows the essential elements: revenue, expenses, and profits. Be sure the Income Statement appears in accrual form and has a Percent of Income column. Adding this column is an option in Quickbooks™, a program your accountant most likely knows inside and out; therefore, asking the accountant to add this column should be a straightforward request.

Once you have the correct report, look at the profits at the bottom. Remember, your Income Statement appears in accrual form, so the figure for the bottom-line of profit represents a theoretical figure. It assumes that you will collect all the invoices you've created and then pay all the bills you currently owe. Hopefully, these are valid assumptions. However, in business, it is not always easy to collect on every invoice. Still, operate under the assumption that you will receive payment for the products and services you provide.

On the bottom line, review the Percent of Income column. You will see a dollar amount and a percentage figure. The dollar amount represents profits for the period that the report covers, and the percentage figure represents the portion of revenues that are your profits.

When you see the percentage figure, it indicates what percent of revenue equals profit. Another way to understand this point is to see that the percent figure shows what amount of each dollar coming into the business is your profit. A 20% Net Profit figure means 20 cents of every dollar coming in is profit. A negative 5% Net Profit means that every dollar of revenue coming in is a loss of five cents.

It is critical to understand both figures, as they will show you whether or not you are on the right track. Over time, both the dollar amount and the percentage figure will fluctuate, but with practice, you can make sure the dollar amount continually increases. The percentage figure may decrease, while the dollar amount may — and hopefully will — increase. For example, if you invest in additional payroll while you grow, you might see the percentage figure decrease and the dollar amount increase.

Important: Keep in mind that it is much better to have 20% of $1 million versus 100% of $100,000. This lesson was important for me to learn. I had a maximum income of $250,000 at one of my former businesses, but at the peak of that company's success, I earned $250,000 each month; that amount is 12 times "the maximum income."

Don't fret if the data on the bottom line of the Income Statement seems discouraging. We'll improve everything one Pillar at a time.

The next piece to review is the Gross Profit. About one-third from the top of the report is a line called Gross Profit. Again, there are two numbers. One is a dollar amount, and the other is the Gross Profit Margin (GPM). The dollar amount should change regularly, while the percentage number should always stay the same.

If your GPM changes more than a percent or two, you most likely recorded inaccurate data. You can expect GPM to increase as time goes by, because product and service deliveries should become more efficient and costs due to volume should decrease.

Revenue. The fun part of the Income Statement is the top line. Sales figures excite many businesses, and rightfully so. After all, as someone once said, nothing happens until there is a sale.

Break the sales figures, or revenue figures, into groups to show where you receive revenue. For instance, if you have a restaurant with dining room sales, banquet hall sales, takeout sales, and delivery sales, each group needs a separate list within the Revenue section.

When you review your Income Statement and the Percent of Income column, you will see the breakdown of your sales as a percent of the total. This way, you can determine how one group is doing in comparison to the others.

Remember, accrual accounting will allow you to list all sales that occur in the reporting period, whether or not the company has received funds. The Income Statement is a document of theory. It assumes that what is on the Income Statement will occur, and in most cases, it does. If we have unpaid invoices from clients, we deduct them after determining the client won't pay.

COGS or Variable Costs. The total for Variable Costs is on the line above Gross Profit. It is the amount subtracted from the top-line revenue number. The percent shows 100% minus your GPM. In other words, the sum of your Gross Profit and Variable Costs equals the top-line revenue. This area can be confusing for business owners who don't have a background or education in accounting. Print your Income Statement. Then, look at your actual numbers for each of these sections to understand your figures. It will add meaning to the Income Statement.

Expenses/Fixed Expense. Let's look at Fixed Expenses, which appears as just "Expenses" on most reports. Yes, there is a dollar amount and a Percent of Revenue (Income) number. Both figures can change. Over time, your total for Expenses will increase, and Percent of Revenue will decrease, because you only have one rent to pay, one CEO to pay, one receptionist to pay, one business coach to pay, and so on. As revenue increases, the percent of income to cover the CEO cost will reduce.

Now, address the details of the Income Statement. Once you have reviewed Net Income, Fixed Costs, Gross Profit, Variable Costs, GPM, and all other figures, consider the Income Statement complete.

Balance Sheet. Think of this document as the report that shows what would happen if everything ended today. If every customer paid what they owed you, and then you repaid every debt you owed and sold everything you had, the final amount would be Owners Equity. It is the same concept as equity in your home. The Balance Sheet keeps track of all assets and liabilities (i.e., debts), and the result is equity.

Assets. The Assets section of the Balance Sheet lists resources a business owns, including cash in bank accounts, accounts receivable, deposits the business has for things like inventory purchases or rent, and everything that belongs to the business from computers to furniture to vehicles. It also encompasses Goodwill or the intangible, yet valuable assets of a company, such as a brand name and image. The brand value becomes significant as a company goes global. Brands such as Google, Amazon, Ford, Gucci, IBM, Disney, and KFC all value their brand worth billions of dollars on the Balance Sheet. Initially, your balance sheet won't have an entry for brand value or Goodwill. As you grow and merge or acquire companies, a portion of the value you and your accounting team places on the acquisition will go toward Brand and Goodwill. Be sure your CPA firm knows everything about what your company does and what your company builds. Frequently, businesses forget about the value of items that the business develops. They often have significate value and increase your company's Equity, which is a positive thing.

Liabilities. The Liabilities section of the Balance Sheet shows a company's debts. This section is like the mortgage on a house. The total dollar amount owed to the bank is the liability. Each payment you make goes partly to interest and partly to the liability or debt. Here, the business records everything from unpaid bills to outstanding payroll to upcoming taxes. Long-term lease payments, including rent and equipment leases, appear here as "Long-term Liabilities." When a business correctly records liabilities, it might look like a colossal figure, because it accounts for all debts, even those that the business cannot pay for a long time. For example, the section might include loans toward which the company makes small monthly payments. That information is not a big deal on a Cash Flow Statement, but it might look intimidating on a Balance Sheet. Again, don't overly concern yourself with the figures. Just be aware of them and work to improve each area over time.

Cash Flow Statement (Historical)

Where did it all go? Every business asks that question at one time or another. Money flows in and out, and sometimes, a bit of money remains in the end. The Cash

Flow Statement shows how the inflow and outflow of cash look historically.

The Cash Flow Statement is a straightforward report. It is a summary document that shows the cash inflow from sales of goods, sales of stocks, loans, and payments the business receives. The report shows what the business paid and where those payments went. For example, it shows expenses, debts, and even stock the company repurchased.

The business should use a Cash Flow Statement each month. Remember, as the owner of the business, you are the pilot of the airplane. The pilot must watch the instruments, so you must watch the financial statements.

In the first days of a new month, my clients share financial statements from the previous month with me. Afterward, we review the numbers together for about an hour. Initially, this experience is educational.

However, clients eventually need only a quick review here and there, because they know how to review the financials before we meet. As you learn more about your financials, your confidence as a business owner will grow.

WHAT NOW? ACTION STEPS.

- ❏ What monthly strategies does your business have in place to analyze and make decisions based on your monthly financial statements?
- ❏ How do you need to improve your financial pillar to accurately find the inadequacies and find the "bad data"?
- ❏ What terms do you not understand from the many that were presented in this chapter? Write them down and work on understanding them fully.
- ❏ Write down the top five priorities for your business in the financial pillar that need attention. Discuss with your accountant or business coach and develop strategies to put in place.

CHAPTER 7:

THE TEAM PILLAR

Team is the Key

As an acronym, the word team might stand for "Together, Everyone Achieves More." I learned that concept during my coaching career. Leverage is another way to understand the team. With a great team, you have a better chance of building a successful business. If the team cannot overcome challenges or becomes the challenge itself, your business will face difficulties and have trouble reaching its full potential.

Here is what I learned about leverage with my technology consulting practice. Initially, I worked 30 to 50 hours a week and charged about 40 hours per week to earn $5,000 weekly. It worked out to be $250,000 per year before taxes. I had no paid vacations, no paid sick time, no career advancement plans, and no quarterly or annual goals. I also did everything — from marketing to sales to operations to finance. Over a couple of years, I learned to hire people, and my best time was to teach the team to do what I was doing. The company earned more and more revenue, and after a couple of team members were in place, my income exceeded the $250,000 I had earned when I was a one-person company.

Important: Do you think no one can do what you do better than you? You're correct. Your brain, experiences, and intuition are yours. You are unique, and from your perspective, you can't expect anyone to do anything better than you. Of course, other people feel the same way and have their views on the matter. In truth, there frequently is someone else who can do what you do and do it better than you. To achieve more success, you will want to hire people to do tasks. They won't be as good as you, and that is okay. The more people you hire, the less tasks you will do, and the more revenue the company can earn. As you learn how to leverage team members and become a CEO, you will see revenues and profits escalate.

Hiring for Success

"What is more important when hiring a team member: attitude or skills?" I ask clients this question, and I usually get the same response. Often, the answer is attitude. I agree that attitude is most important. However, when we place an advertisement for a position, we receive resumes. These cannot show attitude. They only show skills. Within this system, we trick ourselves into hiring for skills first and attitude second. Let's discuss that point.

Hire on deselection, not selection. I learned the deselection process from ActionCOACH™, and now, I teach it to all my clients. The process begins by becoming comfortable with decreasing your workload by 80%. You won't waste time rummaging through resumes, because you will hire on attitude first and leverage technology to do it well.

Here is an idea we teach. Have telephone interviews first. Focus the conversation toward life lessons, not specific skills. You can teach skills later. If candidates have a positive attitude, continue the interview process with them. Focus on attitude first, and you'll acquire a talented team with a positive outlook.

Rock-Star Training Program

So, you hired on attitude first and skills second, and you acquired a strong team. If you don't work hard to keep team members, they will find a better place to work. The best people pick where they work, not the other way around.

Now, it's time to decide how well to train your team. Do you want staff members to become rock stars, or do you want them to remain mediocre? (Always choose the former, not the latter.)

I recently heard the founder of DocuSign Mark TK talk about how the companies with the best teams win.

Remember that the competition will get and keep the best team unless you can do it sooner and better.

Day 1: You could focus on mundane tasks, such as having a new employee fill out paperwork, pointing out areas of the office, and asking the new employee to read the employee manual. But, you want to give a good impression. So, instead have balloons and a gift basket ready on the new employee's desk. Then, give the person an in-depth agenda for the first few weeks of training that you'll call the Rock-Star Training Program (RSTP). Later that day, have a variety of coworkers join the new employee for lunch and talk about life outside of work. By the afternoon, everyone will have met the new team member, who will begin seeing that everybody works hard and loves what they do. By the end of the day, the new employee will know all the job's perks. Plus, he or she will have a chat with the direct supervisor and answer the question, "How do you define success?" Finally, the day ends with another gift for the team member's spouse.

Day 2: The new employee will spend the day with the business owner or the direct supervisor. Together, you'll discuss the company's history and vision. This day helps the new person feel at home. At this point, the company's culture and long-term vision become clear. The new employee begins to see that this company is the best in which to work, so he or she can't wait to give value to the company.

Days 3 to 5: The new employee receives an introduction to all the company's departments. Make sure everybody has a clear understanding of the roles they supervise and the tasks they manage. Clarify all the routes to career advancement or lateral movement. Help new employees see that they, themselves, control their destiny.

Days 6 to 10: The new employee will interact with other team members to train and learn the ropes. Remember, you want rock stars, not mediocre team members. At some point in these first weeks, invite the new team member to bring his or her significant other to a happy hour or dinner to meet other team members.

Days 11 to 15: The intense training happens during this time. There will be tutorial videos to watch and documents to read. Interactive learning is the best way to handle this type of instruction, so include it as much as possible. Also, scatter some quizzes and tests throughout the training.

Day 16 and Onward: The new employee will continue to grow in the role and become a valuable asset to the business. Add training opportunities, and schedule times to talk to the employee about how he or she is adapting to the role.

Should I Strive to Be a Manager or a Leader?

A manager manages resources, while a leader leads people. Have you heard that saying?

Running a business means you get to be the leader. You can lead your people into battle every day, and with great inspiration, positive motivation, and clear vision, you can expect exceptional results.

Mr. John Maxwell once said, "Leadership is getting people to do what you don't want to do." Later, he explained that leadership is knowing that you are not the right person to do something that needs to happen and then getting someone else to do it.

Leadership is necessary whether your business has a thousand employees or one. A business owner must be a great leader to grow the company. Does that mean the word "manager" is something to throw out? Of course not. We need managers to oversee the day-to-day operations and keep track of the KPIs. Not all employees can manage on their own, and managers can help to motivate and supervise them.

Imagine what it would look like if everyone was self-managed. It would change the way businesses hire. Having a self-managed staff would be the number one request from business owners. If a job candidate admitted during an interview that self-management was not in his skillset, he likely would not get the job.

Perhaps parts or even most of your team manages itself well. However, the fact remains that there always will be someone on the team who is not self-managed. Conceivably, that person has yet to acquire the skills, because no one ever tried to teach him or her the right strategies.

Should this topic be something the manager teaches directly? Would anyone opt to attend a class on how to be self-managed if the manager taught one? No, probably not. Most people would say they already are self-managed. Therefore, the manager needs to figure out other ways to help everyone become self-managed.

Let's discuss how self-management looks. We can find one example of self-management at the world's largest tomato processor, Morning Star. This company is a shining example of strong profits, great growth, low employee turnover, and stunning innovation. Leading the company's list of innovations is its approach toward self-management.

A Forbes article described Morning Star's Self-Management Program this way:

"No one at the company has a boss. Employees negotiate and set individual responsibilities with their fellow workers. Everyone can spend the privately held company's money without budgetary constraints. Nobody carries a title, and there are no promotions. Compensation at the largest tomato processor on the planet is peer-based."

Morning Star's strategy might not work for all organizations. Still, how can businesses promote self-management? As in most innovation, leadership should begin at the top. Here are some rules for self-management.

Honor your word. Keep promises you make. Generate trust by being dependable first and foremost. Increase productivity by creating good work habits and rejecting bad ones. Have discipline and keep yourself accountable without other people having to tell you what to do. Have a good work ethic. Do what it takes to complete the work. Remember that good manners count. Be courteous, thoughtful, and respectful.

KPIs are a great way to keep everyone self-accountable. If all team members were to post their KPIs for the day on a whiteboard, they would likely become self-accountable, and hopefully, self-managed. The manager would still need to create appropriate KPIs or at least confirm that the team created appropriate and attainable ones. Sometimes, when a manager leaves the team to its own devices, the staff sometimes creates KPIs that are nearly impossible to reach. Then, when people fail to reach those KPIs, they kick themselves and fall in a downward spiral.

Follow the "SMART" criteria to create suitable KPIs. In doing so, you make sure the KPI has a smart purpose for the business. The KPI must be measurable and achievable, so that the company can observe its progress. Plus, the KPI must be results-oriented and time-sensitive. That way, the company can see the outcome and value within a specific, relevant period.

Leadership and management are both necessary skillsets, and until the company splits the roles, the leader must be the manager and vice versa. The manager will remain the leader until the team reaches about eight people, at which time the business owner will become the leader or find a different leader. If you are the business owner, you can manage or lead depending on what your skills are and how you can grow your team and business to reach goals.

Choosing between managing and leading your business can be difficult, but you must do both to improve the bottom line. Let's use the Pareto Principle of 80:20. Initially, the business might require 80% management and 20% leadership. As the company and staff grows, the needs trade places to 80% leadership and 20% management.

You are most likely better at either management or leadership. However, being a strong manager is essential while you first grow a company, whereas being a strong leader becomes more and more important as time goes by. In the short term, you must be the person who can take care of the resources and handle the business every day. Refer to the section on behaviors to understand yourself and your team. Identify the leadership traits you have or want to have, and build upon your skills.

WHAT NOW? ACTION STEPS.

- ❑ How does your plan look for hiring? Do you hire for success and attitude?
- ❑ After reading about the Rock-Star Training Program, what improvements do you need to improve upon? Design your 10 to 15 day training program if you do not have one documented.
- ❑ Determine if you are stronger as a leader or a manager and decide if this is a fit for your business at this time.
- ❑ What areas do you need to improve in managing your team? List at least five areas that you can begin to examine and change. If you get stuck ask one of your team members.

CHAPTER 8:

EXPANSION

I started my technology business in a spare room in a suburban house in Houston, Texas. Over time, the business grew and added team members. We moved to an office. Then, we opened a second office in Dallas, Texas. Later, we opened a third office in Charlotte, North Carolina. In this way, we expanded a small town business to three cities in two states.

Unfortunately, the second and third offices failed. Back then, I thought the failure was a lack of sales. Today, I know it was marketing that failed, not sales. It was Pillar 1, not Pillar 2. I didn't understand marketing at that time and I didn't yet have a marketing system. Consequently, the offices outside of Houston failed due to insufficient sales, which occurred because of insufficient leads.

If you build all the Pillars of the business properly, you will expand. But you will be more successful than I was with my technology business since you will expand the right way.

Ask yourself and your team, "Was last year all it could have been?"

Use these four steps to achieve more success

Looking back is a critical task to complete. Take it seriously. Looking back, when done correctly, can illuminate what the future might hold. For example, consider what your business looked like last year. Was it a record-breaking year? Were sales flat or declining? Did your industry expand, contract, or stay the same? How did your company's sales compare to your competition's sales? Answer these questions, and then follow the simple four-step process below to help you review the past to improve the future.

Step 1: Thoroughly understand where you are today.

Step 2: Decide to stay where you are or change where you are.

Step 3: Create a list of actions to take to change your current position.

Step 4: Execute those actions until you reach the position you desire.

Step 1, thoroughly understanding where you are today is pretty straightforward. Maybe you see the business grow at a pace that exceeds inflation, and you see maximum profits and take regular vacations while the team handles customers. Or maybe you don't. If you don't, are you the person working the hardest in your business? Are the most sales — or even just the big sales —

dependent upon you? Are you not where you should be considering your experience, your knowledge, and your industry? Take a hard look at your situation and figure out where you are today.

In my opinion, the most difficult step is Step 2, deciding whether to stay or change where you are. Step 2 is the one that seems to challenge my clients the most. Although it should be a simple step, it is challenging, because we must make a serious decision. Do we really want to change? Answering honestly is the challenge. Do you want to change? The answer is only yes or no. There is no room for "maybe," and you cannot rationalize this one.

When you create the list of actions in Step 3, you might include a variety of items. You might be familiar with some of them. For example, let's say sales are below what they should be, and the problem is either insufficient sales, because of a lack of leads, or insufficient leads, because of poor marketing. Pick an issue to improve, and then create a list of actions to take to improve the situation.

If you choose marketing, look at your SEO and website. Also, look at where your best customers have come from in the past. Is it time to add another marketing element to the mix, because other marketing processes have slowed down or stopped working?

If you have a good number of leads, but don't seem to be turning them into sales, review your sales scripts, unique sales propositions, and guarantees. Maybe a referral strategy worked well in the past, so you never established a great sales process, because new customers came from referrals.

Today, referrals are slowing down and your other leads are not converting, because you don't have a good sales process. Are you selling the old way, which was about your product or service's benefits and features, instead of finding a new way that focuses on what's in it for the customer? Creating actions to take can be as simple as reading books on marketing and sales or watching video tutorials on the internet.

The most manageable step can be Step 4, performing the actions you listed and repeating those actions until you reach your desired position. Taking action is easy when you have a good "why" or reason. You want to provide a good life for your family. You want to make more money this year. You want to donate to a charity of your choice. Simply feeling like you want to do better, because you know that you can, is a great reason. Maybe you see a mountain and want to climb it. That reason is good enough for some people, especially those who want to be the next Michael Phelps or Bill Gates of their industry.

Making decisions in Step 4 is easier with help from a coach or mentor. In fact, many successful people acknowledge their coaches and mentors. As a business coach myself, I find it rewarding beyond imagination to see the results that clients achieve. When the student is ready, the teacher appears. Are you ready?

Lead the Way

Business owners must know this information. Do you?

As a business grows, the owner learns about the market, the team, the product or service, and much more. The single most challenging thing for every business owner is not what they do know, but what they don't know. Thus, the business owner should investigate what he or she does not know.

Education is the best way to learn what we don't know. Educate yourself by reading books, listening to others, and experiencing the world around you. Some education methods are faster than others. A quick way is to learn from someone else's experience. A slow way is to experience things on your own. Both methods work, but one takes longer than the other. Also, consider education methods that work well for you and your staff.

As a leader in the community, I am entirely about helping businesses learn what they don't know as fast as possible. I help my clients grow fast and continue to have fast growth. Learning through experience takes a long time — sometimes generations — while learning from others can take minutes. Save yourself time and learn from others.

Here are great ways to educate yourself so that you can achieve results in your own business.

1) Leverage other people's experiences by reading about them. It takes a few hours to obtain years of experience.

2) Create a list of things you don't know, and then learn or think about them. Here is an example list.

   a. Your cost to acquire a new customer
   b. Your lifetime value of a customer
   c. Your average dollar sale
   d. Your lead to conversion rate
   e. Your retention rate of customers
   f. Your retention rate of team members
   g. Your personal lifetime goals

3) Ask someone to hold you accountable for achieving results.

WHAT NOW? ACTION STEPS.

- ❑ Use the four-step process to review how you could expand and plan for next year's growth for you personally and for your business.
- ❑ Step 1: Thoroughly understand where you are today.
- ❑ Step 2: Decide to stay where you are or change where you are.
- ❑ Step 3: Create a list of actions to take to change your current position.
- ❑ Step 4: Execute those actions until you reach the position you desire.
- ❑ Using the three ways of educating yourself, choose one or all three of them to implement.

CHAPTER 9:

BYE BYE OR BUY?

Is it time to say goodbye or good buy? Every business will face one of these three changes when a business owner moves on from the company.

In the best case, the business owner sells the business when it is prime and ready for sale. Doing so allows the business owner to reap the rewards of having grown a successful business.

In the second scenario, the business owner sells or gives the business to someone, maybe a family member, when the business is no longer in its prime. Instead, the business owner is just ready to move on from the company for reasons like age or health. Therefore, the change in ownership is necessary to keep the business afloat.

In the last case, the business owner passes away, and someone else must sell it or get rid of it. This one happens, because the business owner — and maybe the team — did not plan properly.

The first option is the best. The second option is imperfect, but sometimes understandable. The last option usually occurs when the owner is in denial about too many factors. The scenario that happens is in the hands of the current business owner and sometimes the team.

Every business can and should plan for the first and best option: to sell when the company is ready for sale at a time that secures the most significant reward possible for the current owner. It doesn't mean the business must achieve 100% market share, be the top-ranked business in its industry, or become a public company. All it means is that the business needs to be at a level of success where the current owner feels comfortable moving on and leaving a new owner in charge.

The best way to understand this stage of the business is from the buyer's "What's in it for me" or "WIIFM" for short. Act as if you are someone who wants to buy a business. As a buyer, you want a company with a level of success that is worth paying for, because the hard work to get the business to the point of sale already has taken place. Purchasing a business in this state will save you a significant amount of time, because the business already will have gone through some of the toughest challenges that start-up businesses face.

There are tons of buyers out there who would put their hard-earned money toward the purchase of a successful business that way. It happens every day.

Too often, business owners underestimate the value of the business in the eye of the buyer. For example, I regularly meet business owners who own companies they started, because they wanted a job. The business owner grew the business over some years. Now the brand has a strong reputation, the team has dozens of staff members, and the marketing and sales processes include strategies that work well. Plus, the business owner has a personal income of six or seven figures.

The business owner mistakenly thinks no one would buy the business, so I bluntly let the business owner know that thinking that way is wrong. Many people would market this business and sell it for a large sum of money, which would allow the owner to retire and enjoy retirement.

For each of the Five Pillars, there is a checklist to follow to grow the Pillars properly. Use the checklist as an outline for selling the business to ensure you get the maximum sales price at the current stage of the business.

Indeed, you can grow the Five Pillars into a large and successful company. Then, the business owner can make a smart decision about when to sell. He or she will have done everything necessary to prepare the business and the next best step will be to sell.

Often, a business only needs between 12 to 18 months to maximize the sale price. Start where the buyer starts. If you were going to buy a business, what would you want to know first? Maybe after reading the past chapters of this book, you realize the most important part is the financials. So, you ask, "How is this business doing?" But, what you mean is, "Show me the money."

Therefore, you need to have proper financials ready to share with your prospective buyer. The buyer will provide these reports once you secure an arrangement and sign the non-disclosure agreement (NDA) and other legal documents that you and your attorney will have created in advance. Legal documents like an NDA are necessary, because selling a business involves sharing confidential information that you want to keep private.

Your accountant or CPA firm would have helped you create financial documents, such as the Income Statement, Balance Sheet, and Cash Flow Statement. You would adjust these documents to show "add-backs," which help the business owner see what the real profits will be when the new owner takes over.

An add-back is something that is added to the net profit figure, because the new owner won't have those expenses. Review each add-back to determine its validity.

All financial statements need to be accurate. The prudent buyer will look at bank records, deposit statements, and every single financial transaction that occurred in past years. I've evaluated businesses to purchase in the past, and one had a value of more than $1 million. While I considered the purchase, I reviewed financial documents and compared the financials to the bank statements. I even selected deposits at random and called the bank to confirm the validity of those deposits. It annoyed the seller, but I had to guarantee the accuracy of the value.

What is the next area where a buyer wants to have confidence before purchasing the business? It depends on the business for sale. Usually, it is the probability of customers staying. Do customers buy weekly from this business, or do they pay monthly dues, annual dues, or biannual dues? A pizzeria might have customers who buy weekly. A professional networking organization might have monthly dues. A dentist's office might see clients every six months. A veterinary clinic might not see the same people for two or three years.

Know the probability of customers staying so that you can calculate the purchase price and the value of the business. If the clients tend to buy once and leave, that means there is a continuous need for a marketing machine to generate the leads and clients. Look at the customer base and read the customer reviews. Compare the number of repeat customers to the number of new customers or the "churn" as some people call it.

One business I looked at buying had a retention rate of only 50%. That meant that it lost 50% of its customers every year. The business had to replace half of the customers in this subscription model business to have the same revenue each year and overcome that 50% churn.

As you review the Five Pillars, you will see ways to improve individual Pillars, improve the documentation of those Pillars, and improve the goals and plans for each Pillar as well.

Remember, prepare for an exit by planning for at least 12 months before putting the business on the market. This time will allow the company to get ready and then sell for the maximum amount possible at that stage.

WHAT NOW? ACTION STEPS.

- ❏ Which of the three scenarios are you in the case of moving on from the business?
- ❏ Can you name three or more areas in which you are in denial or not planning for the end of the business?
- ❏ What action steps are you taking to prepare for the sale of the business?
- ❏ What can you identify in your financials to determine some add-backs in the consideration of selling the business?
- ❏ How much time are you taking to analyze the Pillars of the business to prepare a strategy to sell?

CHAPTER 10:

THE SALE PRICE

The amount someone gets for a business is dependent on many factors. One is just the ability for the seller to negotiate. This book won't address this skill. There are many resources available on negotiation, which is necessary for the success of many Pillars, including the Team Pillar and the Sales Pillar.

Multiples are how much a company sells for, so you want to sell for the most multiples possible. There are limits to multiples, because at some point, the buyer could build your business for less than the purchase price even when factoring in the time component.

At my tech business, I was shocked and disappointed to learn that the multiples a services business received were only two or three times the annual profits. This multiple reduces if the current owner is heavily involved in daily operations.

Picture a consulting business where the product, which is the team of consultants, goes home every day, and the owner still has direct involvement in management and sales. What chance of survival does the business have after the owner leaves the company? The probability is low for companies in some industries, such as the technology services industry, because the buyer's WIIFM is not good enough. That type of business would take a hit if it were still small, with fewer than 100 employees and less than $10 million in revenue. As this type of business grows, the multiple grows, because the probability of additional success increases.

Say you have a business that earns $1 million per year. You pay yourself a $150,000 annual salary, so you have a taxable income of $150,000 per year.

But in the end, your business might sell for $450,000. That equals two times the profits when you replace yourself with a manager who gets a $75,000 salary.

Here is the math:

Your $150,000 salary minus your manager's $75,000 equals $75,000 of profit. Add the original taxable income of $150,000 to get $225,000.

The buyer can assume this equation will continue for two years without much risk. Therefore, you can sell the business for $450,000.

This simple example includes no specific assets, such as products the company developed, technical devices the company uses, or other resources that might increase the sale price.

If you have a manufacturing business, the multiple can be higher. You might see 20 times the profits or even a multiple of revenue, which is better.

Again, consider the buyer's WIIFM and the buyer's perception of the sale price. A wide range of factors can change the final value. Strategizing with a business broker, a business consultant, or a business coach can help you determine the best sale price.

In a middleman type business that sells other manufacturers' goods, the sale price could be high, because the risk potential could be low. Therefore, the growth potential could be high. Amazon is a great example. This one-time online bookstore didn't write books or rely on one author, and it didn't sell to one type of customer. Today, it sells for $16 to $18 per share or $300 million.

Amazon went public in May of 1997 with the company valuation of $300 million and only had sales of $15.75 million; a 19x multiple of revenue. "Amazon.com is the leading online retailer of books," the company said succinctly in its S-1 filing. At the time of this writing, Amazon's market cap is just shy of $1 trillion (now with a P/E ratio of 179 which is 179 times the company's annual earnings).

The company incurred net losses of $5.8 million and $3 million in the fiscal year ended December 31, 1996. So, a company that was sold for $300 million with losses of almost $6 million didn't sell for a multiple of profits, it instead sold for a multiple of revenue and sold at 19 times the revenue number. This is because of the interpreted low risk and extremely high growth potential. Even as this is written, the expectations that Amazon will continue to grow and earn exponential amounts is why the company is trading stock at almost 200 years of the current profit amounts.

Here is how you can determine what your business is worth. Pay a company to do a business valuation. Be honest with the numbers. Ask the valuation company what factors will boost the value. Ask them who might pay the most for your company, because the purchase of your business added to their business has significant value.

A great example might be an insurance company that buys a property-management company, which already manages 10,000 single-family homes. There is a standard valuation, but there is also an added value for the insurance company, which could convert a certain percentage of the property management company's customers into buyers of its insurance products. In this way, one plus one is worth more than two, because of synergy.

Maximize the sale price by giving yourself and your team at least a year to grow, document, and price the business, and then find an appropriate buyer.

During that year, decide if and how you want to approach the team with the news of the sale. Do you tell them? What do you say? Will everyone quit? Let's look at some of the answers together.

What, If Anything, Should You Tell the Team?

Selling the business at the right time for the right amount requires help. Leveraging the team stabilizes a successful exit and allows the new owner to succeed.

Almost no business owners tell their entire staff that they are selling the business. Most don't say a word until they complete the deal and sign the paperwork. Then, when there is no looking back, they begin to inform the staff. However, just because most business owners keep quiet does not mean it is always the right practice. It is just common.

Usually, no one finds out, because the business owner fears what might happen if the entire team were to learn that the current owner planned to leave. We have discussed fear in this book, and you will recall that it is the reason many businesses do many things, but it is not always a smart reason. In this case, that point is arguable. Let's look at factors you can consider while you determine who to inform of the sale and what to say.

Business Continuity. At some point, the business should be able to continue without the business owner. Although people don't talk about that point much, it is reality.

Strive to help the person who buys your business. You want to ensure there is continuity, which requires most of the existing team to remain.

How that happens can occur in a variety of ways. Let's start with the assumption that senior leadership and management need to stay for at least six months to a year. They will need to have a good reason to stay and that reason might be a financial reward, a promise of a bright future with new opportunities, or a chance to work with a savvy new business owner.

I recommend the book: *Built to Sell: Creating a Business That Can Thrive Without You,* by John Warrillow. In this book, a fictional character named Alex works to sell his advertising business. Alex has trouble selling the company, because of various reasons that you discover throughout the story. Along the way, Alex engages with his senior team members to prepare the business for sale and gives them a substantial bonus for staying on board and the new owner gives them a future that includes massive expansion.

Your business broker, coach, or consultant can advise you. Listen to the advice you receive from people who have experience in this area.

When I sold my companies, almost no one knew about the pending sales except the business owners and one or two staff members who helped us prepare for and complete the transaction. However, today I would engage senior leaders to maximize the company's value and I would tell them about the new owner's vision. Plus, I would offer a financial reward when the business sold and I would give them a bonus to stay on for a minimum amount of time — most likely six months to a year.

What about the taxes on the sale price? Won't we owe lots of money to the government for selling? Let's discuss those points.

Cash, Please — Maybe

Because the sale of a company is usually a taxable event, you should talk to your CPA firm about the tax consequences. Depending on the current capital gains taxes, you should consider specific strategies. These may or may not decrease the tax payments, so you must contact your tax advisors to discuss options. Here are some strategies that might help.

Get paid later, over time. Depending on the risk you feel exists by getting paid, along with difference in tax payments, you could defer getting paid in different tax periods (years). Picture it — during the year of the sale of the business, you earn $350,000 by summer. You pay taxes at the maximum level, perhaps in the 34% tax bracket, and you plan to sell the business by winter. You could agree to receive payment for the sale in the next tax year when your tax bracket reduces to 20%. Maybe you will receive $1 million for the business, so you agree to take payments over 10 years at $100,000 per year, which keeps your tax rate 20%. Together, you and your CPA firm determine that this strategy is smart, because it saves you 15%, or $150,000. It all depends on the numbers and timing.

Get paid in shares of stock. A public company might acquire your business. If so, you can receive shares of stock as payment. This strategy could keep the taxes lower than they would be if you received a cash payment. You might also believe the stock will increase in value. Selling the shares would be a taxable event, but you might be comfortable with it, because the share price would be significantly higher by the time you sold. Again, evaluate this idea thoroughly with the help of your legal team and CPA firm.

Get paid in other assets. There are a few transactions that the US Government IRS Tax Code allows to occur without any tax payment. Most tax specialists and some business brokers know these strategies. Depending on the value of the assets when you sell, you might use this strategy to decrease taxes. I'll repeat one more time that you need to evaluate this idea with your legal team and CPA firm's help.

Risk and Reward

This specialized area is important. You must understand that there is a risk you will not receive a payment from the new owner. If the new owner defaults, the business might even return to you in whatever shape it exists.

This situation can be horrible. You worked hard for years to build a sellable business, and you agreed to sales terms you thought were good. Regardless, the business nearly went bankrupt and came back to you in shambles. Now, the only recourse you have is to retake control. In this disaster, you receive improper payment, the business tanked, and you returned feeling depleted and mentally checked out, because you thought you had moved on from the company.

The reward for payment terms must justify this risk. If an enormous company buys your business and pays you in stocks that carry restrictions for, say six months, you can protect yourself from disaster with proper stock strategies. Plus, you can rest assured that there is a slim chance of the enormous company going under in six months. Therefore, this sale might be a calculated risk worth taking.

Be sure you and your accountant and legal team evaluate the risk and reward for any of the payment terms. Sell when you feel comfortable.

I had a negative experience with new owners who destroyed the business I sold them. It took lawsuits to get them to pay me. It was a painful learning experience that I share with my clients as a cautionary tale about selling a business. I did not employ a financial and legal team, and I did not evaluate the risks and rewards the right way. I didn't know what I didn't know, and that blindspot was financially and emotionally damaging.

Of course, I don't want to scare you away from selling a business. Yes, there are complexities in selling a business, collecting the payments, and paying the taxes. However, this situation is still better than the alternatives of selling, because you risk never selling and watching the asset become worthless.

The effort is worth it. It is a skill you'll not have the first time, but you can leverage other people's skills and learn along the way. Plus, you might learn to enjoy the sales process. If so, you can begin a new journey of buying, fixing, and selling businesses.

WHAT NOW? ACTION STEPS.

- ❑ On a scale of one to five, with five being super confident, what is your current confidence level for negotiating the price you desire in the sale of your business? If it is under five, what actions can you take to improve in this mindset?
- ❑ What are the multipliers for increasing the value of your business? If you do not know, make a plan to hire someone that can help you figure this out.
- ❑ What is the for-sale date to begin your plan of action to sell your business? Start working backwards with the actions needed to begin the plan.
- ❑ Who have you invited to be on your advisory team to discuss the selling of the business? How have you described their role and action steps to make it happen?

CHAPTER 11:

LET'S DO THAT AGAIN!

We've made it to the rinse-and-repeat stage of The Five Pillars. Here, you know how to improve the Five Pillars and you enjoy the challenge. Now, you can create tremendous wealth by buying, fixing, and selling businesses. Venture Capital Firms make the world's most notable deals, which are in the category called Mergers and Acquisitions. They look for businesses that are flat or declining. Then, they team up with strategic companies for synergy. This time, one plus one is not just more than two; it's 20 or more. We'll start small, and you can work your way up to the large mergers.

The Flipping of Businesses

Buying a business. Remember that you risk capital — yours or someone else's — when you buy a business. Be wise about taking this route, as it can lead to troublesome situations if you aren't careful. But you will be careful, right? So, let's take a look.

You are shopping for a business. The simplest of the considerations is how much you can afford. Start small and work your way up after each successful flip. Don't aim for the grand slam home run on the first try; rather, focus on getting a good base hit.

Perhaps you will look for a $10,000 business that is struggling even though there are plenty of customers, and the labor force is plentiful. Make the first one as easy as possible. Only give yourself six to 12 months to complete the flip. Don't hold it any longer, and don't buy something you necessarily love. Instead, buy something you want to fix and sell. Keep as much emotion out of it as possible.

Let's create a process to follow

Step 1: Research. The first step is to learn what is for sale. Use the internet. You might be surprised to find great business opportunities close to home or in a neighborhood near you. Search "businesses for sale" on the internet to help you find what you want or contact a business broker through a website. Even a classified advertisements website can be a place to start.

Print a list of every business that meets your budget. It does not matter what the business is at this point. If you could make it happen financially, print it out. Eventually, you will create a spreadsheet with a variety of columns of data, including business prices, revenues, customer counts, market sizes, average dollar sales, and a dozen other factors. For now, know the sale price and the type of business. Also, do not sign anything to get data. We'll get there soon enough.

Step 2: Refine. Be realistic as you refine possibilities. For example, if you see a dentist's office for sale, and you aren't a dentist, or your state or area requires a dentist to own a dentist's office, this sale is unrealistic for you. Yes, you could make it happen, but it would be an uphill battle every day. Until you are an expert at buying, fixing, and selling businesses, I recommend looking elsewhere.

As you review your list, which could have a hundred or more options, categorize the possibilities into three categories: I, II, and III. The categories correspond with the level of specific education and knowledge you and the team members need to run this particular business.

Here are a couple of examples: A pizzeria would go in category I. It would be easy to train the team, and many people could fill the jobs. A dance studio would go under category II, because you would need dance instructors who had skills that took years to develop. An animal clinic would be in the category III section, because the veterinarian who led the team would need doctoral degrees to work with the animals.

Take a look at this table of additional examples.

Business	Category	Reason
Day Care	I	Although state regulations can be complex, the team required can quickly get necessary certifications.
Restaurant	I	Define operations, and then most people with a high-school education could join the team and operate the business.
Technology Services Company	II	You would need professionals with certifications and degrees to make this business successful. (I know, because I've done it.)
Bookkeeper	I	It might be easy to find staff members, but it takes time to teach them how to enter data, print reports, and keep information accurate.
Automobile Dealership	III	From the financing to the insurance this is a large endeavor. It is a great business model once you have learned all you can.
Fitness Studio (e.g., a yoga studio)	II	This is a simple business except for finding the team members - what is good is there are LOTS of team

		members available, thus the "almost Simple" ranking
Engineering Firm	III	Everyone employed is degreed. Some have advanced degrees. Salaries will be high, and projects will be sophisticated.
Pet Grooming and Supplies Shop	II	Finding and training associates should be straightforward, but it may take extra time to find groomers with the education, experience, and skills to succeed.
Retail	I	This business requires great management to be successful, and team members need to learn about sales and operations. However, it should be manageable.

Step 3: Create Your Rules. Some people might think this step should be first. However, in your first go-around at flipping businesses, you need to learn the rules before creating them. Therefore, I put this step third. Your rules will be the top 20 things that make a difference to you in your decision to buy or not to buy a business. I've included my first set of rules as an example. Some relate to the amount of work you do "in" the business, how fast you would fix and sell the business, and how simple the work is. Considerations also include your desired return on

capital, whether or not there are repeat customers, and the level of demand for the product or service.

Step 4: Eliminate and Select Your First 10 Rules. Review the list of possible businesses that fit your financial means. Circle 10 that meet 100% of the rules and put them on a shortlist. It's okay if you can't get to 10, but do not go over 10. Sort the list according to price from lowest to highest. Now, it's time to create a spreadsheet.

Step 5: Gather All Data. Most people dislike this step, but it is crucial. Begin a thorough analysis of each business. As you begin the analysis, you may have to sign an NDA, which you should review before signing, probably with your attorney. You need the data, and an NDA might be necessary before the seller or agent can release it. You must gather the data, and you must do the analysis. Remember, keep emotions out of it. Enter the data on the spreadsheet, and then create columns for businesses with more data than others. Be sure to collect and note all critical KPIs for the businesses as well.

Step 6: Start the Meetings. You already sorted the possible acquisitions according to price from lowest to highest. Now, meet with the business owners or their agents. These meetings can be informal, but they are necessary, because they help you and the other parties get to know one another. During the meeting, take pictures if you have permission. Never be afraid to ask questions. Here are some common questions to ask.

1. Why are you selling?
2. What is the minimum down payment you will accept?
3. How do you contact past customers?
4. What will you do after you sell?
5. Do any of your close friends or family members work here?
6. Who has the final say about whether or not to sell?
7. How do you feel about selling?
8. How long will you assist the new business owner after you sell?
9. What has been the biggest challenge in the business so far?

If you were starting the business today, but knew what you know now, what would you do differently?

There are many other useful questions. Ask anything you want. You don't know where the business buried the skeletons, which means negative things, and there will be some. After all, the business owner is selling the business. Looking at the bottom, you are not going to find shining stars. Instead, you are looking for a business that you can buy at a low price, invest a little time and money into, and then sell for a significant profit. Ask questions. Take notes. Know that you are learning this process. You'll do it again and again, and you will get better each time.

Step 7: Select One. Review the spreadsheet of data to see which of the opportunities seems like the best to buy, fix, and sell. Look for businesses where you can make significant changes just by improving marketing. Look for businesses that have not leveraged existing customers for additional sales or referrals. At this size, businesses often struggle, because they do not use the database of past customers. They fail to send newsletters with special offers or ask customers for referrals. You're going to put offers and discounts in emails, letters, and other forms of communication.

For example, I often forget to book haircut appointments in advance. By the time I return to the barbershop, I look like a shaggy dog, because it has been about six weeks. However, I'd probably get haircuts more often if the barbershop scheduled my next appointment while I was there or offered me a deal to book in advance or a discount to give a referral. Therefore, the barbershop could increase sales from the same customer by implementing rebooking strategies or buy-again offers.

Each business will have multiple opportunities for improvement. The best for you will be the one where the improvement strategies are ones you already are good at implementing.

Step 8: Negotiate. This step can and should be fun. If you aren't yet comfortable negotiating, take classes, read books, and role-play negotiations. Consider the seller's pain factor. Is the seller losing money each month? Is the seller working every day of the week? Does the seller involve a spouse in the business, but not pay appropriately? If these things are happening, you don't have to negotiate at all. Instead, keep asking questions, and the seller might drop the price. The seller will remain eager. After all, here you are, thinking about buying the business and giving the seller a way out.

I once found a pizza place for sale at $60,000 on Craigslist. The owner wanted to sell directly without a broker, so it was easy to email the owner, schedule a phone call, and then visit the business. I asked many questions, such as the ones I mentioned above. I promised to review the numbers and to get back to the owner in a few days. As I was leaving the store, he said, "If you can buy the business in 45 days, I'll sell it for $45,000." I said, okay, I'll be in touch, and I left. He dropped the price $15,000 (25%) without me even asking for a better price.

I called back a couple of days later and asked due diligence questions to prove things like the sales numbers, average dollar amount of sales, number of customers, and so on. The seller agreed to bring receipts to prove the sales and costs were what he had reported, and within two weeks, he brought me bags and boxes of sales receipts and expense receipts. It was a mess. I felt sorry for the seller. He and his wife were working every day that they were open, and they brought their five-year-old son to work, too. They were living comfortably on the profits. However, they could not reinvest any funds into marketing, repairs, or team members. They were in a bad situation, and it wasn't improving.

I had my assistant tabulate the receipts, and I discovered revenues were higher than what the seller had reported. Rarely are the numbers better than what a seller first says. I found he had been paid cash on 25% of his sales. The person who had sold him the business had done it that way, so the seller working with me had kept doing it. The seller had explained the situation to me when we first talked about the company's value, but he never said the business was worth more, because of it. The seller didn't know how to grow a business and didn't know how to sell a business either.

Within 30 days of due diligence, I spent time sitting in the parking lot and watching the phone ring. I counted the orders that the company delivered, and the orders people picked up. I even had some friends try out the pizza. Finally, I was ready to make an offer.

When I called to say I wanted to discuss the price and make an offer, the seller said, "I'll take $25,000," which left me almost speechless. I had been ready to offer $35,000. I knew that the resale value of the used equipment alone was more than $40,000, and I was even willing to go up to that amount if necessary.

I determined that if I put the extra $15,000 toward marketing and hired an excellent team to run the store, I would be able to sell the business for $125,000 within six months and earn about $75,000 on my $50,000 investment. My math also showed that the business would make up to $35,000 in profits after expenses over those six months. It was around a 250% ROI with little risk, and I wouldn't have to do anything except sign papers, transfer money, hire a manager, and outsource the marketing. With the new low-ball, self-offer of $25,000, the ROI went up to 275%. So, I agreed to the deal.

However, I was reluctant. Sometimes, things that seem too good to be true are too good to be true. In the process of drawing up the paperwork, I hesitated. I wondered what I was missing. I couldn't figure out why the seller was so desperate to sell that he would drop the price to $25,000.

So, I delayed. Days turned into weeks, and 45 days later, we still had not reached a deal. The seller called multiple times to ask where we stood, but eventually, he knew I wasn't going to buy. He was upset, and rightfully so. I apologized and said I wasn't comfortable yet and needed more time.

The C in my four-quadrant behavior pattern profile kicked in. I overanalyzed and procrastinated, and I didn't make a decision. After 30 days, I came to my senses and sent the seller a text message to say I was still interested.

However, he replied that he had already sold the business for $60,000, his original asking price.

Yes, someone else saw the deal and realized it was good enough at $60,000. I had been too slow to buy it at $25,000. Indecision killed the deal. It would have been a good deal for me, and at the time for the seller, because he desperately wanted out. We all make mistakes, and my lesson here was to make decisions quickly once I have the information. Even if it had been the wrong decision, I could have made other decisions to correct it.

Step 9: Paperwork. Minimize your risk by having an attorney draw up the purchase agreement, which likely will be something called an Asset Purchase Agreement (APA). You don't want to buy any debt or liabilities that exist. You only want to get the assets. Your attorney is best suited to handle this type of purchase and prepare all the documents necessary. Do not try to save money here. Just hire a great attorney.

To make the sale legal and safe, you need the APA and other documents, such as the Non-Compete Agreement, Non-Disclosure Agreement, Asset List, and Bill of Sale. Sellers should have an attorney, but frequently won't, because the situation is dire and they need to sell. Once you complete the paperwork, you are the proud owner of a business you can flip. The clock is ticking. It is time to get to work, fix what you can, and sell as quickly as possible.

Step 10: Hand Over. You will likely receive a few days, weeks, or months of training from the previous business owner. Make sure the manager is there for the training. You, as the new business owner, should not be learning too much, as you are not going to be working "in" the business as much as the manager. Remember, you are not supposed to fall in love with this business. You are supposed to fix it and sell it as soon as possible.

Step 11: Prepare for Listing. Remember the checklist for preparing a business for sale? Get that out, and work to complete as much on that checklist as possible, so that you can maximize the sale price and then sell and profit from the fix.

If you have a small business, such as a pizza parlor, you will probably sell for less than $200,000. In that case, listing the business by yourself and handling the inquiries might be okay. The broker fee eats into your profits substantially at this stage. Remember, if you are good at buying, you can be good at selling.

As you prepare the business for sale, keep in mind the new buyer's WIIFM. As the size of the businesses you flip increases, the ease of operations becomes more critical for the absentee business owner. If the business is worth $200,000 or so, people buying into the business are probably purchasing a job and feel happy to do so. They will pay one to three times the annual earnings on the business. They will know that they are likely to increase the earnings, and profits will continue to increase for years. When it is time to sell, you will earn a higher value, because the business will be earning more, be more systemized, and easier to operate.

Buying, fixing, and selling businesses is an excellent activity when you reach the investor stage of building wealth. With practice, you will secure bigger deals, because your knowledge and confidence will grow.

There is always a buyer if there is enough WIIFM. If you aren't sure how much WIIFM a business has, go back to the drawing board before signing a deal or putting a business up for sale. You must have a sale price in mind for the fixed business, and you must learn about the planned profits and ROI during the due diligence stage.

Never expect miracles to happen. Instead, plan to turn mediocre businesses into great ones. You can earn a great income from the business flipping strategy. Just be ready to learn along the way.

Remember, Brad Sugars says, "The more you learn, the more you'll earn." You've learned a lot about growing businesses in this book. Now, it's time to go out and make it happen. As I always say, knowledge becomes valuable when you act upon it – time to start acting.

WHAT NOW? ACTION STEPS.

- ❑ Have you considered buying a business? If yes, who are you considering to partner with you on this adventure?
- ❑ What risks have you written down and planned for in the consideration of buying a business? Make a list and discuss with your advisory team.
- ❑ Examine your list of risks and create action plans for your first purchase of a business.
- ❑ Using the process described in this chapter, decide the category and reasons for the businesses you are researching to purchase.
- ❑ What WIIFM have you documented into scripts to begin the process?
- ❑ Make a list of obstacles in this process and discuss with your advisory team or your coach.

ADDENDUM

FIVE PILLAR CHECKLIST

These checklists are to be used as an outline to create a plan for the business to ensure you get the maximum sales price at the current stage. You also can use the checklists of each of the Five Pillars to leverage your growth and success if you have become complacent in any given area. By making smart decisions, having a plan, and a coach to hold you accountable for the actions in the checklists, you will be prepared.

Finance Pillar

- ✓ Financial statements in order on a monthly basis — Balance Sheet, Profit and Loss Statement
- ✓ Break-Even Analysis — calculation of the sales level at which a business recovers all its costs or expenses
- ✓ The Business Performance Forecast — a budget that identifies predicted future performance of the business
- ✓ Cashflow performance of the business
- ✓ Reporting monthly to any funds, loans, or banks will need to be submitted to the different entities.

Marketing Pillar

- ✓ Monthly marketing cost for acquisition of new customers
- ✓ Measure lead generation sources, conversion rate, average dollar sale, and know your profit margin
- ✓ Unique selling proposition
- ✓ Guarantee
- ✓ Lifetime value of your customers

Sales Pillar

- ✓ Documented sales process with seven or more steps
- ✓ Mindset or skill set training
- ✓ Communication training

Operations Pillar

- ✓ Vision and mission statement
- ✓ Culture points
- ✓ Organizational chart
- ✓ Positional contracts for team members
- ✓ Common goals
- ✓ Documented how to system manuals
- ✓ Management systems

Team Pillar

- ✓ Strong leadership and management with passion and responsibility
- ✓ Team roles and responsibilities are defined

- ✓ Key performance indicators for all members of the business
- ✓ Rules of the game — hard and soft rules for all members of the business in place and documented
- ✓ Consistent documented appraisal system

ACKNOWLEDGMENTS

None of this would have been possible without my best friend, business partner, and life partner, Tim. He has stood by me during struggles and successes and continues to provide the daily support needed to continue to grow and help me to help others do the same.

Thank you to my parents and family for all your support.

Thank you to all my foreign exchange student children, it has been so wonderful sharing our lives and cultures together.

My local and global teams deserve a huge thank you — locally at N3 Coaching, their edits and never-ending support to get to the finish line has been amazing; and globally, my extended team are great at asking questions, great at providing answers, and amazing to just be there to listen.

A very special thanks to ActionCOACH™ and all the life-changing experiences needed to become a successful coach. None of it possible without the founder, Brad Sugars, who inspires and motivates me to achieve more almost daily.

Another special thank you another of my many mentors, Dr. Marshall Goldsmith; Thank you for your examples, leadership, and pushing me to get this book complete and then to pull out all my resources to help people get their own copy. Without the creation of the MG100, there would not have been the "what's your date" question by the members; huge thank you to the MG100 for causing me to take action to get the book done.

Thank you to my thought coach Traci Duez. Without having the thoughts that help me move forward, I wouldn't have been successful in this business — everyone needs a thought coach and Traci has been a miracle worker.

Thank you to every client who has the confidence to ask for help, and then to take action on the mentoring; without your action, our words, and conversations are wasted — keep taking action.

Thanks to everyone at Elite Online Publishing and MyHart Communications for bringing this book to life.

There are so many super-supportive people who have helped mold me (and re-mold me) to be who I am today, and who I'm becoming in the future — thank you for your efforts and for your reminders for me to work harder as there are many more people to help. Although I would love to say each of your names individually, I'd be certain to leave someone out, and thus this is for you — THANK YOU!

Finally, thank you to all those business owners out there who are working hard to make a living, as well as working hard to leave a legacy. Owning a business is hard work, and when you do it the right way, the rewards are limitless — keep up the hard and rewarding work!

ABOUT THE AUTHOR

Doug is an international public speaker, profit-strategist, and award-winning business and executive coach, with multiple years of winning national and global ActionCOACH™ awards, beginning his first entrepreneurial experience selling holiday greeting cards door-to-door. This early drive for success led him to become a very successful business owner, now on his 9th successful business.

Having been the coach for more than 200 business leaders, Doug has had the rare privilege to work in a diverse range of business industries, to name a few: automotive, technology, food service, real estate, franchise, medical, veterinary, and oil and gas — and with an equal number of executives!

Doug earned his degree in Management Information Systems and International Finance from the University of Houston. Soon after graduating, he started his own award-winning, rapid-growth company, which grew to more than 60 employees generating more than $25 million in sales with profits exceeding $250,000 per month.

After semi-retirement at 42, he was enticed to buy a business coaching franchise to teach others what he had been teaching himself for 28 years. From an inauspicious start as the 1,181st franchise owner across 60 countries, Doug reached #1 franchise within four years, becoming the fastest inductee into the ActionCOACH™ Hall of Fame. More recently, Doug won the "Marshall Goldsmith First 25" Award out of 12,000 applicants, an honor that included a seat at the table and professional association with Marshall Goldsmith.

Having been the owner and manager of three multi-million-dollar companies, Doug understands the challenges, pressures, and pleasures associated with being your own boss. He diligently has worked as a consultant, coach, trouble-shooter, and director while also enjoying a wonderful journey! As a business coach the opportunity to facilitate and assist other business owners and entrepreneurs to achieve amazing results is his mission.

Doug was professionally trained by multi-millionaire, author, and world-class entrepreneur, Brad Sugars. With the support of ActionCOACH™ global resources, Doug's coaching, training and development programs are world class.

Doug's strong belief is that having a certified business coach is the single most positive investment a business owner can make in themselves and for their business.

Doug Winnie

N3Coaching, LLC

Certified Business and Executive Coach, Author, Speaker
6300 W Loop S, Suite 502

Bellaire, TX 77401

DougWinnie@BusinessBlindspotsBook.com

Recession/Pandemic BONUS

Implementing the systems in this book
will put you ahead of the competition even during
challenging times.

FREE BONUS

Download the Recession/Pandemic Business Checklist:
BusinessBlindspotsBook.com

CPSIA information can be obtained
at www.ICGtesting.com
Printed in the USA
LVHW080710260121
677447LV00045B/91/J

9 781513 660462